Modern Chinese

Modern Chinese

A BASIC COURSE

by the Faculty of

PEKING UNIVERSITY

Dover Publications, Inc.
New York

Published in Canada by General Publishing Company, Ltd.,
30 Lesmill Road, Don Mills, Toronto, Ontario.
Published in the United Kingdom by Constable and Company,
Ltd., 3 The Lanchesters, 162–164 Fulham Palace Road, London
W6 9ER.

This Dover edition, first published in 1971, is a revised
republication of the Introduction and the first thirty lessons
from the second, 1963, edition of *Modern Chinese Reader*,
originally published by the "Epoch" Publishing House, Peking
(first edition: 1958).
This book is sold separately, and also as part of a package
(entitled *Modern Chinese: A Basic Course*) which also contains
three audiocassettes (Dover catalog number 99910-6).
The Publisher's note to this English edition gives more information on the cassettes and further bibliographic details.

International Standard Book Number
(text and cassettes): 0-486-99910-6
International Standard Book Number
(text only): 0-486-22755-3
Library of Congress Catalog Card Number: 78-169835

Manufactured in the United States of America
Dover Publications, Inc.
31 East 2nd Street
Mineola, N.Y. 11501

PUBLISHER'S NOTE

This book contains the Introduction and the first thirty lessons of *Modern Chinese Reader* (second edition, Peking, 1963), which was compiled by the instructors of the Chinese Language Special Course for Foreign Students in Peking University.*

It was felt that these first thirty lessons comprise an excellent self-contained introduction to Mandarin Chinese as it is spoken in Mainland China today. The first twelve lessons deal with phonetics, tones and pronunciation (eight theoretical and four practice lessons). The grammar lessons follow.

In the original edition, no translations were provided for any of the grammar example sentences or exercise sentences ("Texts") from Lesson 13 on. All these sentences have been translated specially for the present edition.† On the other hand, the original edition repeated all the phonetic and grammatical rules—that is, all the basic text—in Chinese, paragraph by paragraph (for the use of teachers in China). In this edition the Chinese version of this material has been omitted and only the English version is given.

The Vocabulary (glossary) appendix of the original edition has been abridged to include only the words in the first thirty lessons. The pronunciation exercises of Lessons 1 through 4 have been abridged.

The transcription system used in this book is the official one of Mainland China (see the last paragraph of the Introduction). For those readers who are acquainted with one or both of the two most important earlier transcription systems, Yale and Wade, a comparative table has been provided on pages xvii and xviii.

Though complete in itself and suitable for home as well as classroom study, this book will be most valuable if used along with the

---

*Despite the title, it is a grammar, not a reader. The original publication is in two volumes and contains 72 lessons and several appendixes.

†The publisher is grateful to Miss Nancy Duke Lay for checking these translations and making helpful suggestions.

audiocassette set of the same name, being published concurrently. The cassettes are based on the book, and contain (in Chinese only) the Exercises of Lessons 1 through 8 (which include every possible sound and syllable of modern spoken Mandarin), the New Words and Simple Sentences of Lessons 9 through 12, and the New Words and Texts of Lessons 13 through 30.* The corresponding cassette sides and bands are indicated in all these places in this book.

*The original record set, entitled *Records in Spoken Chinese*, manufactured by the China Record Company, distributed by Guozi Shudian (China Publications Centre), Peking, consists of eight ten-inch 33⅓-rpm discs, covering all 72 lessons of the original grammar book. The Dover set consists of three audiocassettes, covering the first thirty lessons, the pronunciation exercises of Lessons 1 through 4 being abridged to match the new text.

CONTENTS

INTRODUCTION

The Chinese language (or the Han language) is the chief language of China, and also one of the most popular and developed languages in the world.

China is a country of many nationalities, and has a population of six hundred million, about 94% of which are of the Han nationality. Each of the national minorities has its own language. The Chinese language is the language of the Han nationality, and also the common social language used among all the nationalities.

The Chinese language, according to present data, consists of eight principal dialects: the Northern dialect, the Kiangsu-Chekiang dialect, the Hunan dialect, the Kiangsi dialect, the Hakka dialect, the northern Fukien dialect, the southern Fukien dialect and the Kwangtung dialect. Above 70% of the population who use the Chinese language speak the Northern dialect. The Northern dialect district includes, in fact, the wide area north of the Yangtze River, the tract of land to the south of the Yangtze River, the west of Chenkiang and the east of Kiukiang, the four provinces of Hupeh (excepting the south-east corner), Szechwan, Yunnan and Kweichow, and last of all, the north-western part of the Hunan province. It is seldom found in the world that so many people of so wide a region speak one and the same dialect. The grammar of all the dialects is fundamentally the same, the majority of words are the same, and only the pronunciation is rather different, but in spite of that, there exist among the various dialects some corresponding phonetic relations. The present condition of the spoken Han language may be described as follows: though the various dialects are still in use, the Chinese people are taking measures to spread the popular language with the Peking speech sounds as the standard so as to unify gradually the various dialects and form a common national language.

The "ancient literary language" (文言) of the Han nationality, which was once universally used in China for so long a period, must have become established on the basis of the spoken language, but it gradually deviated more and more from the spoken language. Hence, there appeared later a new type of written language, which directly recorded living speech, and kept close to the spoken language all the time. This is what we now call the "colloquial language" (白話), which is the source of our present national language in writing. All the works written in the "colloquial language" are, generally speaking, based upon the Northern dialect. At the same time, a branch of the Northern dialect, which represented the local speech of Peking, gradually become the means of social intercourse in the various dialect districts, and was called the "Mandarin language" (官話). The May 4th movement in 1919 stood for writing in the colloquial language and against writing in the ancient literary language, and destroyed the authoritative position of the ancient literary language. As a result, the common language of the Han nationality became gradually unified in its written and spoken forms. The term "popular language" (普通話) was adopted instead of the "Mandarin language". Since the founding of the People's Republic of China in 1949, the written language has become closer to the "colloquial language", and a fundamental union of the written and spoken languages is thus brought about; while the spoken language is further developed.

Because of various historical reasons, the Chinese language did not reach a total unification till now. But a basis has been established for the unification of the Chinese language, that is, the formation of a popular language, based upon the Peking speech sounds as the standard sounds, the Northern dialect as the basic dialect and modern classic works written in the colloquial language as grammatical models. The modern Chinese, which we purpose to teach, is just such a standard language.

Here are some of the chief characteristics of modern Chinese with respect to speech sounds, grammar, words and characters:

Speech sounds (1) The predomination of vowels. Every character, used in the Chinese language, is a syllable by itself. The syllable may consist of a single vowel, a compound vowel or a vowel preceded or followed by a consonant; but a single consonant can never form a syllable by itself, and so it cannot represent any Chinese character. e. g.

hàn (I) yǔ (2) kě (3) ài (4)

(The Chinese language is very charming.)

These four syllables (four characters) are formed respectively by a single vowel (2), a compound vowel (4), a vowel preceded by a consonant (3) and a vowel between two consonants (1).

(2) Tones. Every syllable representing a character, has its definite tone, e. g. "mǎi" (to buy) is pronounced in a falling and rising tone, and "mài" (to sell) in a completely falling tone. The difference in tone makes for the difference in meaning, though both have the same sound elements.

(3) Aspiration and non-aspiration. Whether the beginning consonant of a syllable is aspirated or unaspirated is quite essential for ascertaining the meaning represented by the syllable, e. g. the different meanings of "bǎo" (to have eaten enough) and "pǎo" (to run) are determined by the aspiration and non-aspiration of the beginning consonant of each syllable.

Grammar and words (1) Uniformity of syntax. The word order in Chinese is very important. For example, 我帮助你 (I help you) and 你帮助我 (you help me) are opposite in meaning. 他念書 (he reads a book) cannot be changed into 書念他. 一朵香花兒 (one fragrant flower) is a word group, while 这朵花兒很香 (this flower is very fragrant) is a sentence. A modifier is usually put before that which is modified, e. g. 白馬 (a white horse), in which 白 is an adjective modifier and 馬 the central word or the word modified, and 慢慢兒地走 (walk slowly), in which 慢慢兒地 is an adverbial modifier and 走 the central word.

(2) Particles. Particles are considered a kind of weak or form word in the Chinese language. No particle possesses any concrete meaning. It cannot be used as any sentence element, and therefore cannot form any sentence by itself. Particles are used chiefly for expressing grammatical relations: they may help words in forming grammatical constructions (such as structural particles) and may express sentence moods (such as modal particles) when they are used after words and sentences.

(3) Characters and words. In Chinese, a syllable is a character in writing. There are monosyllabic words and polysyllabic words in Chinese. A monosyllabic word is represented by a character, e. g.

人 rén (man),
来 lái (to come),
好 hǎo (good).

But there are exceptions, e. g. 花兒 (flower) consisting of two characters are pronounced as one syllable (huār). Most of the polysyllabic words are dissyllabic ones, each of which is represented by two characters, e. g.

人民 rénmín (people)

幸福 xìngfú (happiness)

我們 wŏmên (we, us)

Besides, there are also words of three syllables and four syllables.

(4) Simple and compound words. From what has been said above, it is clear that a word may be represented by one character, two characters or more than two; but not every character can form a word. 1. There are characters which can each form a word, e. g. 人 (man). 2. There are characters which may each express a bit of meaning, but cannot stand alone as a word, and can only be a part of a word, e. g. 語 and 言; but these two characters can be combined into a word with a definite meaning: 語言 (language). 3. One character, which can be a word by itself, may, in combination with another character, form another word, and the second character sometimes may form a word by itself, such as 鉄路 (railway), or it may not, such as 人民 (people). 4. There are some characters which only appear in one word, such as 葡萄 (grapes), for neither 葡 nor 萄 can express any meaning by itself, and therefore cannot form another word with any other character. The words given under 1 and 4 are simple words, and those under 2 and 3 are compound words. There are various formations of compound words, and the few instances given here are used only as illustrations. For the sake of clearness, the contents of the above four points may be summed up in the following table:

	Simple words					
Characters {	葡	萄	鉄	路	人	民	語	言
			Compound words				

Chinese characters: The writing symbols of the Chinese language, the characters, have a history of more than three thousand years, according to excavated evidence. Notwithstanding the fact that the Chinese characters originated from a kind of hieroglyphs, they have already advanced far ahead of the stage of hieroglyphs, e. g. from these two ancient characters 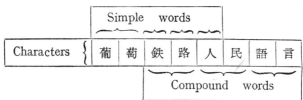 (the side view of a man) and (the side view of an elephant), we can see what they symbolize, but this pictorial form is lost in the same two characters in modern writing, 人 and

象. Most of the Chinese characters indicate shape and sound, that is, one part of each character represents the sense and the other part the sound, e. g.

油 yóu (oil)　氵 (meaning water, representing the sense)
　　　　　　由 ("yóu" representing the sound)
桐 tóng (tree of tung oil)
　　　　　　木 (meaning wood, representing the sense)
　　　　　　同 ("tóng" representing the sound)

But owing to the change of character writing and speech sounds, the sound part of a great number of characters has almost lost its function and no longer represents the sound and tone of the character, e. g.

1. 江 jiāng　(river):　工 gōng
2. 鴿 gē　　(dove):　合 hé
3. 筒 tǒng　(tube):　同 tóng
4. 念 niàn　(to read):　今 jīn
5. 圈 quān　(circle):　卷 juàn
6. 問 wèn　(to ask):　門 mén

For the convenience of discriminating and writing characters, they may be divided into two kinds according to their structure. Characters of the first kind are basic characters, each of which consists of a simple unit, that cannot be analyzed, e. g. 人 (man) and 水 (water). Those of the second kind are mixed characters, each of which is composed of two or more than two simple units. The characters of shape and sound belong to this kind. Comparatively speaking, a mixed character seems somewhat complicated, but it is not really difficult as soon as one makes out each component part of the character.

The number of characters is very great (the Kan-hsi Dictionary records 47,021 characters, not counting the alternative forms), but actually those in common use are only about five or six thousand. According to recent statistics, any one who knows 1,556 characters, is actually in command of 95% of the characters in general use.

The Chinese characters have played a brilliant and important role in the long history of Chinese culture. All the splendid ancient classical literature of China is preserved in these characters. In the period of the Chinese socialist construction, the Chinese characters are now used by the masses throughout the country. In the far future, they will continue to exist, and will be studied by many people. But in order to facilitate the popularization of culture and education, the characters are undergoing a reform. In January, 1956, the State Council of the

People's Republic of China promulgated the Plan of the Simplification of Characters. It aims at simplifying the characters composed of too many strokes, and at selecting one form of a character when there are two or more than two forms.

On the 11th of February, 1958, the 5th session of the 1st National People's Congress approved the Phonetic Scheme for Annotating Chinese Characters. This scheme chiefly serves to annotate the pronunciation of Chinese characters alphabetically, to facilitate the teaching of them, to unify the speech sounds and to popularize the common language. Foreigners will find it very convenient to learn the Chinese language and characters with the help of the phonetic alphabet. Teachers and research students of the Chinese language may also consider further possible reforms of the Chinese characters on the basis of the phonetic alphabet.

COMPARATIVE TABLE OF TRANSCRIPTIONS
OF CHINESE SOUNDS

Peking (this book)	Yale	Wade
a	a	a
ai	ai	ai
ao	au	ao
b	b	p
c	ts	ts', tz'
ch	ch	ch'
d	d	t
e	e, ee	e, ê, eh
ei	ei	ei
er	er	êrh
f	f	f
g	g	k
h	h	h
i, yi	i, r, y, yi, z	i, ih, ŭ
ia, ya	ya	ia, ya
iao, yao	yau	iao, yao
ie, ye	ye	ie, ieh, ye
iou, iu, you	you	iu, yu
j	j	ch
k	k	k'
l	l	l
m	m	m
n	n	n
ng	ng	ng
o	o	o
ong	ung	ung
ou	ou	ou
p	p	p'

Peking (this book)	Yale	Wade
q	ch	ch'
r	r	j
s	s	s, ss
sh	sh	sh
t	t	t'
u	u	u
ü	yu, yw	ü
ua, wa	wa	ua, wa
uai, wai	wai	uai, wai
ue	we	wê
üe, yue	ywe	üe, üeh
uei, ui, wei	wei	uei, ui, wei
uo, wo	wo	uo, wo, o
x	sy	hs
z	dz	ts, tz
zh	j	ch

Modern Chinese

Phonetics

Lesson 1

1.1 Vowels: "a", "o", "e", "i", "u", "ü"

The standard speech sounds of modern Chinese are based upon the speech sounds of Peking dialect. There are six basic vowels in Peking dialect: "a", "o", "e", "i", "u", "ü". Here is the pronunciation of these six vowels:

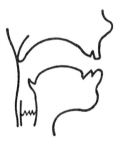

"a": It is produced by lowering the tongue, with the mouth and lips wide-open. The breath comes out freely.

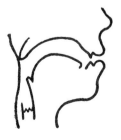

"o": It is produced by keeping the tongue in a half raised position with the back of the tongue towards the soft palate, the mouth a little open and the lips slightly rounded.

"e": It is produced by raising the back of the tongue towards the soft palate, with the mouth half open and the tongue a little lower than in the case of "o". "e" is the unrounded vowel corresponding to the rounded vowel "o".

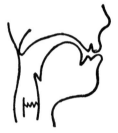

"i": It is produced by raising the front blade of the tongue towards the hard palate, with the mouth a little open and the lips flat, and then letting the breath come out between the hard palate and the blade of the tongue.

"u": It is produced by raising the back of the tongue towards the soft palate, and rounding the lips, with the mouth a little open, and then letting the breath come out between the soft palate and the back of the tongue.

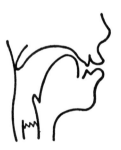

"ü": The position of the tongue is like that of "i", but the shape of the lips is different; the shape of the lips is like that of "u", but the position of the tongue is different; the mouth is kept open as little as in pronouncing "i" and "u". "ü" is the rounded vowel corresponding to the un-rounded vowel "i", and hence "ü" is produced only by keeping the tongue in the same position as in pronouncing "i" and the lips as rounded as in pronouncing "u".

1.2 Consonants: "b", "d", "g"

There are 24 consonants (including two semi-vowels "y" and "w") in Peking dialect. So far as their different positions and manners of pronunciation are concerned, they can be classified into several groups. In this lesson, only "b", "d" and "g" are introduced. These three consonants are unaspirated, voiceless, plosive sounds, because in pronouncing these consonants the passage of the breath is obstructed, and the pent-up air comes out with a pop. According to their positions of pronounciation, "b" is a labial plosive, "d" an alveolar plosive and "g" a velar plosive.

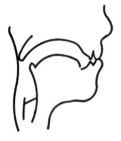

"b": It is produced by pressing the lips together, keeping the breath in the mouth for a moment, and then opening the mouth and letting the pent-up air come out. Don't send forth too much air. The vocal cords do not vibrate.

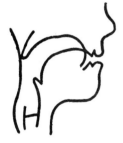

"d": It is produced by raising the tip of the tongue against the gum of the upper teeth and then drawing it away to release the pent up air with a pop. Don't send forth too much air. The vocal cords do not vibrate.

"g": It is produced by raising the back of the tongue against the soft palate, and then drawing it away to release the pent-up air with a pop. Don't send forth too much air. The vocal cords do not vibrate.

1.3 Spelling

Spelling is the joining of two or more sounds into one syllable. e. g.

$$b + a \longrightarrow ba$$
$$g + u \longrightarrow gu$$
$$d + i \longrightarrow di$$

1.4 Tones (1)

The tone is the variation of pitch (chiefly that of its height, rising and falling). The tone rises and falls by gliding and not by bounding. Every syllable in Chinese has its definite tone, and, therefore, tones are as important as vowels and consonants in forming syllables. It is only because of the difference of tones that the meanings of words are different, although the spelling is the same.

There are four tones in Peking dialect. Let us draw a short vertical line to represent the range of the variation of pitch and divide it into four equal intervals with five points. These five points, counted from the bottom to the top, represent the five degrees:

5	the high-pitch
4	the mid-high pitch
3	the middle-pitch
2	the mid-low-pitch
1	the low-pitch

The four tones in Peking dialect are represented by (1), (2), (3) and (4) in the following fig. :

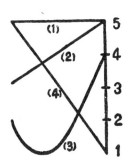

We use the pitch-graphs "⌐, ⌐, ⌐, ⌐ "to represent the four tones. But they can be simplified as follows: —, ⁄, ⌄, ⌏. They must be placed on the vowel (if there is only one vowel) or on the main vowel of a syllable.

In this lesson we only deal with the 1st and 2nd tones.

The 1st tone (55)°is a "high-level" tone. In writing it is represented by the pitch-graph "—" e. g. "gū", "bā".

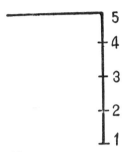

The 2nd tone (35)†is a "high-rising" tone. It is represented by the pitch-graph " ⁄ ". e· g. "dá", "gé".

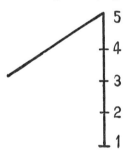

Exercises

SIDE ONE, BAND ONE

1) Read the following vowels: (to be read across)

a	o	e		a	o	e	
a	a		o	o	e	e	
i	u	ü		i	u	ü	
i	i		u	u	ü	ü	
a	o	e		i	u	ü	

° That is, from 5 to 5 on the figure (remaining at level 5).
† That is, from level 3 to level 5 of the figure.

2) Read the following syllables, paying attention to the pronunciation of the consonants: (to be read across)

bo	de	bo	de
ge	bo	ge	bo
de	ge	de	ge

3) Practise the following spellings: (on the record, the columns are read first down, then across)

	a	o	e	i	u	ü
b	ba	bo	—	bi	bu	—
d	da	—	de	di	du	—
g	ga	—	ge	—	gu	—

4) Practise the following spellings and tones: (read across)

ā	ā	á	á
ǖ	ǖ	ǘ	ǘ
bā	bā	bá	bá
dā	dā	dá	dá
bō	bō	bó	bó
gē	gē	gé	gé
bī	bī	bí	bí
dī	dī	dí	dí
bū	bū	bú	bú
dū	dū	dú	dú

Home Work

1) Learn the above exercises by heart and pay special attention to the pronunciation of "o", "e" and "ü".

2) Learn the 1st tone and the 2nd tone by heart, and pay special attention to the pitch of the 2nd tone.

3) Read the vowels and consonants in this lesson as many times as you can, until you are able to write them out from your memory.

4) Write the phonetic symbols in this lesson five times.

Lesson 2

2.1 Consonants: "p", "t", "k", "m", "n", "ng"

(1) "p", "t", "k"

These three consonants are aspirated, corresponding to the unaspirated "b", "d", and "g", and so in pronouncing these consonants, the breath has to be puffed out strongly. The positions of pronunciation of these consonants are the same as those of "b", "d", and "g": "p" is a labial plosive, "t" an alveolar plosive and "k" a velar plosive.

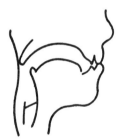

"p": When the breath is about to puff out through the lips, emit as much air as possible. The vocal cords do not vibrate.

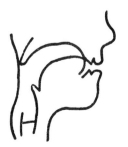

"t": When the breath is about to puff out through the mouth, emit as much air as possible. The vocal cords do not vibrate.

"k": When the breath is about to puff out through the mouth, emit as much air as possible. The vocal cords do not vibrate.

(2) "m", "n", "ng"

These 3 consonants are nasal, voiced sounds. The obstruction formed in the mouth in uttering "m" is like that in uttering "b", the obstruction formed in uttering "n" is like that in uttering "d", and the obstruction formed in uttering "ng" is like that in uttering "g". The difference is that in uttering "m", "n", and "ng" the soft palate must be lowered, thus opening the nasal passage and letting the breath come out from there. According to the positions of pronunciation, "m" is labial, "n" alveolar, and "ng" velar.

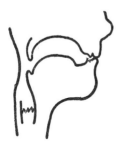

"m": It is produced by pressing the lips together, and letting the air go out through the nasal cavity. The vocal cords vibrate.

"n": It is produced by raising the tip of the tongue against the gum of the upper teeth, and letting the air come out of the nasal cavity. The vocal cords vibrate.

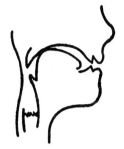

"ng": It is produced by raising the back of the tongue against the soft palate, and letting the air go out through the nasal cavity. The vocal cords vibrate. (Note: "ng" is only used at the end of a syllable.)

2.2 Compound Vowels (diphthongs and triphthongs)

A compound vowel is formed by a combination of two or three vowels. The pronunciation of a compound vowel is starting from one vowel and then moving to or towards another vowel; hence there must be changes in the position of the tongue, the opening of the mouth and the shape of the lips. There are 13 compound vowels:

```
        a  o  e  ai  ei  ao  ou
    i   ia    ie         iao iou
    u   ua uo    uai uei
    ü         üe
```

2.3 Vowels Plus Nasal Consonants

The following 16 compound sounds are spelt by putting nasal consonants after vowels:

an	en	ang	eng	ong
ian	in	iang	ing	iong
uan	uen	uang	ueng	
üan	ün			

The sound values of single vowels and compound vowels deserve special attention. A brief explanation will be given below:

1. "a" and "a" in "ia", "ua" are [A]. "a" in "ai", "uai", "an", "uan" and "üan" is the front-low vowel [a] with the lips unrounded. Strictly speaking, "a" in "ai" and "üan" is similar to [æ], while [i] should be [ɪ]. "a" in "ao", "iao", "ang", "iang", and "uang" is the back-low unrounded vowel [ɑ], and "a" in "ian" is the front mid-low, unrounded vowel [ɛ].

2. "o" or "o" in "uo", "ou" and "iou" is the back-midhigh vowel [o], but a little wider, with the lips not too rounded. The rounding of the lips becomes increasingly less from "o" to "uo", and "ou . [u] in "ou" is a little wider, while the sound of [o] in "iou" is rather weak. [o] in "ao", "iao", "ong" and "iong" is the back-high vowel [ɔ] with rounded lips and wider than [u].

3. "e" is the vowel [ɤʌ] uttered from back mid-high to mid-low with the lips unrounded; it may be written simply as [ɤ]. "e" in "ie", "üe" is the front mid-low vowel [ɛ] with the lips unrounded, while ê alone is also [ɛ]. "e" in "ei", "uei" is the front mid-high vowel [e] with the lips unrounded and [i] is a little wider, while the sound of [e] in "uei" is rather weak. "e" in "en" and "uen" is the high neutral vowel [ə], while the sound of [e] in "uen" is rather weak. "e" in "eng", "ueng" is the back mid-low vowel [ʌ] with the lips unrounded.

4. In ün, ü [y] is followed by a weak [ı] sound.

2.4 Tones (2)

In this lesson we discuss the 3rd and the 4th tones in Peking dialect.

The 3rd tone (214)° is a "falling-and-rising" tone, it descends from the mid-low pitch to the low pitch and then rises up to the mid-high pitch. It is represented by the pitch-graph "✓", e. g. "bǎ" and "nǐ".

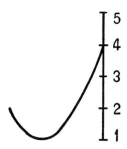

The 4th tone (51)† is a "falling" tone, it falls from high to low. The pitch-graph is "╲", e. g. "tù" and "pò".

° That is, from level 2 through level 1 to level 4 on the figure.
† That is, from level 5 to level 1 on the figure.

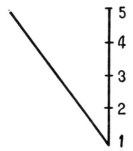

In learning the four tones the following points have to be noticed:

(1) The above figures only indicate the pitch variation of the four tones in Peking dialect. Actually the pitch of human voice is not the same for all persons.

(2) The tone represents the pitch variation, it has no relation to the intensity of sound.

(3) The four tones are different in length, and in analysis, the 3rd tone is the longest, and the 1st and the 2nd tones are longer than the 4th tone.

Exercises

SIDE ONE, BAND TWO

1) Read the following syllables, paying attention to the pronunciation of the consonants: (to be read across)

po	te	po	te
ke	po	ke	po
te	ke	te	ke

bo	bo	po	po
de	de	te	te
ge	ge	ke	ke

bo de ge   po te ke

mo	mo	ne	ne
mo	ne	mo	ne

2) Read the following compound vowels: (**to be read across**)

a	i	ai	a	i	ai
a	o	ao	a	o	ao
o	u	ou	o	u	ou
e	i	ei	e	i	ei
i	a	ia	i	a	ia
i	ê	ie	i	ê	ie
i	ao	iao	i	ao	iao
i	ou	iou	i	ou	iou
u	a	ua	u	a	ua
u	o	uo	u	o	uo
u	ei	uei	u	ei	uei
u	ai	uai	u	ai	uai
ü	ê	üe	ü	ê	üe

3) Read the following compound syllables and pay attention to the difference between -n and -ng: (to be read across)

an	an	ang	ang
en	en	eng	eng
an	en	ang	eng
in	in	ing	ing
uen	uen	ueng	ueng
uen	uen	ong	ong
in	uen	ing	ueng
ün	ün	iong	iong
uen	ün	ueng	iong

an	ang	ong
ian	iang	iong
uan	uang	
üan		

4) Practise the following tones: (to be read across)

ǔ	ǔ	ù	ù	ǔ	ù
bǎ	bǎ	bà	bà	bǎ	bà
pǎo	pǎo	pào	pào	pǎo	pào
kǎn	kǎn	kàn	kàn	kǎn	kàn
bǎng	bǎng	bàng	bàng	bǎng	bàng

děng	déng	dèng	dèng	děng	dèng
pìn	pìn	pìn	pìn	pìn	pìn

ī	í	ǐ	ì
ū	ú	ǔ	ù
mō	mó	mǒ	mò
ǖn	ǘn	ǔn	ǜn
īng	íng	ǐng	ìng

Home Work

1) Learn the above exercises and pay special attention to: 1. the different pronunciation between "b" and "p", "d" and "t", "g" and "k". 2. the pronunciation of "an, en", "ang, eng", "in, uen, ün" and "ong, ing, ueng, iong". 3. the difference between the 2nd and the 3rd tones.

2) Learn all the phonetic symbols in this lesson by heart, until you can write them out from your memory.

3) Write the new phonetic symbols five times.

Lesson 3

3.1 Consonants: "f", "h", "l", "z", "c", "s"

(1) "f" and "h"

These two consonants are voiceless fricatives. In pronouncing them, the passage of the breath is small but not completely obstructed, so that the breath comes out with friction. According to their positions of pronunciation, "f" is a labio-dental fricative, and "h" a velar fricative.

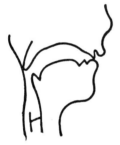

"f"; Press the lower-lip against the upper teeth, and let the breath come out with friction. The vocal cords do not vibrate.

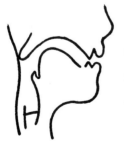

"h": Raise the back of the tongue towards the soft palate, and let the breath rub through the channel thus made. The vocal cords do not vibrate.

(2) "l"

It is a voiced alveolar lateral. It is produced by raising the tip of the tongue against the gum of the upper teeth to stop the air passage, and thus letting the air come out by the sides of the tongue. The vocal cords vibrate.

(3) "z" and "c"

"z" is an unaspirated voiceless affricate, and "c" is an aspirated voiceless affricate. In pronouncing them, the air passage is completely obstructed, then the tip of the tongue moves away a little and the air is let out by rubbing through the narrow channel in the mouth, and so the obstruction and the friction come close together. Both of them are blade-alveolar affricates.

"z": Press the tip of the tongue against the gum of the upper teeth, and let the breath puff out and rub through the narrow channel thus made between the tip of the tongue and the teeth. Don't emit too much air. The vocal cords do not vibrate. "c": The pronunciation of this sound is the same as that of "z" sound. The only difference is that "c" is pronounced with a strong puff of breath.

(4) "s"

It is a blade-alveolar voiceless fricative, and is produced by lowering the tip of the tongue to the back of the lower teeth, and letting the breath rub through the narrow channel between the middle of the blade and the upper teeth.

3.2 The Blade-alveolar Vowel after "z", "c", "s"

The blade-alveolar vowel [ʅ] after "z", "c", "s" is also represented by "i". There cannot be any confusion, because the vowel sound of "i" [i] never occurs after "z" "c", "s" in Peking dialect. This vowel [ʅ] only occurs after z, c, s, therefore it sounds like the voiced prolongation and weakening of the fricative element of the preceding consonant.

3.3 Retroflex Vowel "er (-r)"

This sound is produced with the tongue a little forward from the position of the mixed vowel "e" (the international phonetic symbol is [ə]), with the tip of the tongue turned up towards the hard palate, thus producing "e" sound with a curved tongue "r". In pronouncing this sound, keep the mouth from a little open at first to a little close.

3.4 Components of Chinese Characters (1)

The Chinese characters, the written symbols of the Chinese language, are, in general, constituted of several parts. Each part of a Chinese character is called a "component of the Chinese character" (some components are also characters when they stand by themselves). The components of Chinese characters are composed of a number of basic strokes. Therefore, we should pay much attention to the ways of writing of these basic strokes and the order of the strokes in making any component (or character).

In this lesson, we only deal with the basic strokes of Chinese characters. The following seven basic strokes are the most elementary:

Exercises

SIDE ONE, BAND THREE

1) Read the following syllables, paying attention to the pronunciation of the consonants:

fo	fo	he	he	le	le
fo	fo	he	he	le	le

zi	zi	ci	ci
si	si	zi	zi

zi	ci	si		zi	ci	si
si	ci	zi		si	ci	zi

2) Read the following spellings: (to be read across)

fu	fú	fǔ	fù
hāo	háo	hǎo	hào
luō	luó	luǒ	luò
zāo	záo	zǎo	zào
zān	zán	zǎn	zàn
cāi	cái	cǎi	cài
sōng	sóng	sǒng	sòng
cī	cí	cǐ	cì

3) Read the following retroflex vowel "er":
(to be read across)

er		er		er			
ēr		ér		ěr		èr	
ēr	ēr	ér	ér	ěr	ěr	èr	èr

4) Practise writing the basic strokes.

Home Work

1) Read the first three sections of the exercises several times and pay attention to the pronunciation of "z" and "c".

2) Copy the basic strokes of Chinese characters in this lesson several times.

3) Write the new phonetic symbols and basic strokes of characters five times.

Lesson 4

4.1 Consonants: "zh", "ch", "sh", "r", "j", "q", "x"

(1) "zh" and "ch"

"zh" is an unaspirated voiceless affricate, and "ch" is an aspirated voiceless affricate. In pronouncing them, the passage of the breath is completely obstructed, then the tip of the tongue moves away a little and the air is let through by rubbing the narrow channel in the mouth. The obstruction and the friction come close together. These two consonants are blade-palatal sounds (or retroflex sounds).

"zh": Turn up the tip of the tongue against the hard palate, and then let the breath puff out and rub through the channel between the tip of the tongue and the hard palate. Don't emit too much air. The vocal cords do not vibrate.

"ch": The pronunciation of this sound is the same as that of "zh" sound. The only difference is that "ch" is produced with a strong puff of breath.

(2) "sh" and "r"

These two consonants are also blade-palatal sounds. "sh" is a voiceless fricative and "r" is a voiced fricative.

"sh": Turn up the tip of the tongue near the hard palate, and let the air rub through the channel between the tip of the tongue and the hard palate. The vocal cords do not vibrate.

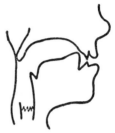

"r": It is the voiced sound corresponding to "sh", and so in producing this sound the vocal cords vibrate. (The blade-palatal vowel [ʅ] after "zh", "ch", "sh", "r" is also represented by "i". There can be no confusion, because the vowel sound of "i" [i] never occurs after "zh", "ch", "sh", "r" in Peking dialect. This vowel [ʅ] only occurs after "zh", "ch", "sh", "r", therefore it sounds like the voiced prolongation and weakening of the fricative element of the preceding consonant.

(3) "j" and "q"

"j" is an unaspirated voiceless affricate and "q" an aspirated voiceless affricate. In producing these two sounds, the air passage is completely obstructed, then it is slowly opened and the air is let through by rubbing the narrow channel in the mouth. The obstruction and the friction come close together. These two consonants are front-palatal sounds.

"j": Raise the front of the tongue to the hard palate, place the tip of the tongue against the back of the lower teeth, and then let the air puff out and rub through the channel between the front of the tongue and the hard palate. Don't emit too much air. The vocal cords do not vibrate.

"q": The pronunciation of this sound is the same as that of "j" sound, except that it should be produced with a strong puff of breath.

(4) "x"

"x" is a voiceless fricative. It is produced by raising the front of the tongue near the hard palate, and then letting the air rub through the channel between the front of the tongue and the hard palate. The vocal cords do not vibrate.

4.2 The Syllabic Construction of Peking Dialect

(1) In Peking dialect, a single vowel, a compound vowel or a vowel with a consonant (whether the consonant stands before the vowel or after) may form a syllable, but a consonant cannot form a syllable by itself. Every syllable has its definite tone. e. g.

è	(饿	hungry)	ài	(爱	to love)
ēn	(恩	favour)	hé	(河	river)
bǎo	(饱	full, to eat one's fill)	shuāng	(霜	frost)

(2) Every syllable is a Chinese character. Therefore, according to the Chinese traditional method of phonetic analysis, the sound of a character may be generally divided into "shēng" 声母 (the consonant at the beginning of a syllable) and "yùn" 韻母 (the rest of the syllable after the consonant). Besides, every character has its proper tone. In "hé" and "shuāng" given in the above examples, "h" and "sh" are "shēng's" 声母, "e" and "uang" are "yùn's" 韻母; "hé" is in the second tone, and "shuāng" is in the first tone. But there are also characters which are composed of only "yùn" 韻母, such as: "ēn" in the above examples.

(3) Every syllable in Peking Dialect consists of a "shēng" and a "yùn". A "yùn" can be a single (main) vowel, e.g. chá (tea); it can also be a vowel plus a medial vowel and a "yùn ending", e. g. biǎo (watch); sometimes it can be a medial-vowel and a main vowel. e. g. shuō (to speak, to say);

or only a vowel and a "yùn ending", e.g. kàn (to see). There
are only three medial vowels: "i", "u" and "ü". "yùn's" can be
divided into four types: 1. those without medial vowel or without "i", "u", "ü" as the main vowel; 2. those with the medial
vowel "i" or using "i" as the main vowel; 3. those with the
medial vowel "u" or using "u" as the main vowel; 4. those
with the medial vowel "ü" or using "ü" as the main vowel.
Any vowel can be a main vowel and any consonant (except
"-ng") can be a "shēng". The combinations of "shēng" and
"yùn" are chiefly determined by the positions of articulation
of "shēng" and the type of "yùn". The following table shows
all the possible combinations of "shēng" and "yùn":

声母 shēng ＼ 韵母类别 types of yùn	1	2	3	4
b p m	+	+	+	−
f	+	−	+	−
d t	+	+	+	−
n l	+	+	+	+
z c s	+	−	+	−
zh ch sh r	+	−	+	−
j q x	−	+	−	+
g k h	+	−	+	−
0	+	+	+	+

"+" indicates that "shēng" can go with "yùn", while
"−" indicates that it cannot.

"0" indicates zero "shēng".

4.3 Four Points about the Ways of Writing

(1) When "i", "u", "ü" and a "yùn" 韵母 beginning with
"i", "u" or "ü" are not preceded by any "shēng" 声母, they

must be written as follows:

> **yi,** ya, ye, yan, you, **yao, yin,**
>
> yang, ying, **yong.**
>
> **wu,** wa, wo, **wai, wei,**
>
> wan, wen, wang, weng.
>
> yu, yue, yuan, yun.
>
> (The two dots on ü are omitted.)

(2) When "ü" or a "yùn" 韻母 beginning with "ü" spells with "j", "q", "x", they may be written as "ju", "qu", "xu", without the two dots on "ü", but when the consonants "n", "l" are followed by "ü", the two dots cannot be omitted, e.g. "nü", "lü".

(3) "iou", "uei" and "uen" are basic forms, but they must be written as "—iu", "—ui" and "—un", when they are preceded by a consonant. The tone-graph is placed on the last vowel "u" or "i" in the simplified forms "—iu" and "—ui", e. g. "niú", "guì".

(4) In case two syllables of which the second one begins with "a", "o", "e" should run into each other and cause confusion in pronunciation, the dividing sign " ' " must be used. e. g.

$$\begin{cases} \text{fáng'ài} & \text{妨碍} & \text{(to hinder)} \\ \text{fāngài} & \text{翻盖} & \text{(to rebuild)} \end{cases}$$

4.4 Components of Chinese Characters (2)

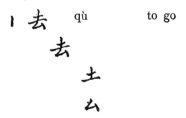

去　qù　　　to go

chàng   to sing

Exercises
SIDE ONE, BAND FOUR

1) Read the following syllables, paying attention to the pronunciation of the consonants: (to be read across)

zhi	chi	shi	ri
zhi	chi	shi	ri
zhi	zhi	chi	chi
shi	shi	ri	ri

ji	qi	xi	ji	qi	xi
ji	ji	qi	qi	xi	xi
ji	qi	ji	qi	ji	qi
qi	xi	qi	xi	qi	xi

2) Read the following syllables and pay attention to their ways of writing:

1. è, ài, ǒu, yǔ, wǎng, yǒng.
2. yōu, wán, yá, yì, yíng, wǒ, wǔ, wèng, yūǎn, yǔn.
3. jǔ, qù, xuǎn, qióng, lǚ, nǚ.
4. huí, wèi, guì, kuí, wěi, liū, qiú, diū, jiǔ, xiù, lún, wén, chūn, shùn, tóng, wēng.
5. ⎰ yīn'àn   陰暗   (gloomy)
   ⎱ yínán   疑难   (puzzle)
   ⎰ míngē   民歌   (folk song)
   ⎱ míng'é   名额   (number)
   ⎰ fáng'ài   妨碍   (to hinder)
   ⎱ fāngài   翻盖   (to rebuild)

3) Read the following dissyllabic words:

1. zhuānjiā	2. qīngnián	3. sīxiǎng
4. yīnsù	5. yánjiū	6. rénmín
7. niúnǎi	8. zázhì	9. diàndēng
10. wèntí	11. fùnǚ	

4) Notice the basic strokes of the following components of Chinese characters and copy them several times:

1	土	一 十 土
2	厶	㇛ 厶
3	口	丶 冂 口
4	日	丨 冂 冃 日
5	曰	丶 冂 曰 曰

Home Work

1) Learn the exercises of this lesson by heart, and pay attention to the pronunciation of "zh" "ch", "sh", "r", "j" and "q".

2) Copy the second section of the exercises, read it aloud.

3) Copy the components of Chinese characters five times.

Lesson 5

SIDE TWO

5.1 Table of the Chinese Phonetic Alphabet

(the names of the phonemes are read on the record)

letters			names	letters			names
printed form		written form		printed form		writtten form	
A	a	$\mathcal{A}$ a	[a]	N	n	$\mathcal{N}$ n	[nə]
B	b	$\mathcal{B}$ b	[pə]	O	o	$\mathcal{O}$ o	[o]
C	c	$\mathcal{C}$ c	[ts'ə]	P	p	$\mathcal{P}$ p	[p'ə]
D	d	$\mathcal{D}$ d	[tə]	Q	q	$\mathcal{Q}$ q	[tç'iou]
E	e	$\mathcal{E}$ e	[ɤ]	R	r	$\mathcal{R}$ r	[ar]
F	f	$\mathcal{F}$ f	[əf]	S	s	$\mathcal{S}$ s	[əs]
G	g	$\mathcal{G}$ g	[kə]	T	t	$\mathcal{T}$ t	[t'ə]
H	h	$\mathcal{H}$ h	[xa]	U	u	$\mathcal{U}$ u	[u]
I	i	$\mathcal{I}$ i	[i]	V	v	$\mathcal{V}$ v	[və] *
J	j	$\mathcal{J}$ j	[tçiə]	W	w	$\mathcal{W}$ w	[wa]
K	k	$\mathcal{K}$ k	[k'ə]	X	x	$\mathcal{X}$ x	[çi]
L	l	$\mathcal{L}$ l	[əl]	Y	y	$\mathcal{Y}$ y	[ja]
M	m	$\mathcal{M}$ m	[əm]	Z	z	$\mathcal{Z}$ z	[tsə]

*The letter ''v'' is used only in spelling the words adopted from foreign languages, languages of national minorities and various dialects.

5.2 Table of the Chinese Vowels and Table of the Chinese Consonants

(1) Table of the Chinese Vowels
(on the record, read as "a o e ê i u ü er")

	tip-tongue vowels		palatal vowels		
	blade-alveolar	blade-palatal	front	central	back
high (close)	-i	-i	i ü		u
mid-high (half-close)				(e)	e o
mid-low (half-open)		er		(e)	
				ê	
low (open)				(a) a	(a)

The blade-alveolar vowel and the blade-palatal vowel are represented respectively by the borrowed letters from Swedish [ŋ] and [ʐ]. "er" may be represented by the international phonetic symbol [ər].

(2) Table of the Chinese Consonants
(on the record, read across, then down)

	unaspirated voiceless plosives and affricates	aspirated, voiceless plosives and affricates	voiced na- sals	voice- less frica- tives	voiced lateral, voiced fricative
labial	b [p]	p [p']	m [m]	f [f]	
alveolar	d [t]	t [t']	n [n]		l [l]
blade-alveolar	z [ts]	c [ts']		s [s]	
blade-palatal	zh [tʂ]	ch [tʂ']		sh [ʂ]	r [ʐ]
palatal	j [tɕ]	q [tɕ']		x [ɕ]	
velar	g [k]	k [k']	ng [ŋ]	h [x]	

5.3 Table of Compound Vowels and Vowels Plus Nasal Consonants

(on the record, read across, then down)

a	o	e	ai	ei	ao	ou	an	en	ang	eng	ong
i	ia		ie			iao	iou	ian	in	iang	ing	iong
u	ua	uo		uai	uei			uan	uen	uang	ueng
ü		üe						üan	ün		

Table of the Speech Sounds of Peking Dialect

(This table is continued on the following two pages. On the record, the columns are read downward, beginning "ba, pa, ma, ...")

yùn shēng	a	o	e	-i	er	ai	ei	ao	ou	an	en	ang	eng	ong
b	ba	bo				bai	bei	bao		ban	ben	bang	beng	
p	pa	po				pai	pei	pao	pou	pan	pen	pang	peng	
m	ma	mo				mai	mei	mao	mou	man	men	mang	meng	
f	fa	fo					fei		fou	fan	fen	fang	feng	
d	da		de			dai	dei	dao	dou	dan		dang	deng	dong
t	ta		te			tai		tao	tou	tan		tang	teng	tong
n	na		ne			nai	nei	nao	nou	nan	nen	nang	neng	nong
l	la		le			lai	lei	lao	lou	lan		lang	leng	long
z	za		ze	zi		zai	zei	zao	zou	zan	zen	zang	zeng	zong
c	ca		ce	ci		cai		cao	cou	can	cen	cang	ceng	cong
s	sa		se	si		sai		sao	sou	san	sen	sang	seng	song
zh	zha		zhe	zhi		zhai	zhei	zhao	zhou	zhan	zhen	zhang	zheng	zhong
ch	cha		che	chi		chai		chao	chou	chan	chen	chang	cheng	chong
sh	sha		she	shi		shai	shei	shao	shou	shan	shen	shang	sheng	
r			re	ri				rao	rou	ran	ren	rang	reng	rong
j														
q														
x														
g	ga		ge			gai	gei	gao	gou	gan	gen	gang	geng	gong
k	ka		ke			kai		kao	kou	kan	ken	kang	keng	kong
h	ha		he			hai	hei	hao	hou	han	hen	hang	heng	hong
o	a		e		er	ai		ao	ou	an	en	ang		

yùn / shēng	2									
	i	ia	iao	ie	iou	ian	in	iang	ing	iong
b	bi		biao	bie		bian	bin		bing	
p	pi		piao	pie		pian	pin		ping	
m	mi		miao	mie	miu	mian	min		ming	
f										
d	di		diao	die	diu	dian			ding	
t	ti		tiao	tie		tian			ting	
n	ni		niao	nie	niu	nian	nin	niang	ning	
l	li	lia	liao	lie	liu	lian	lin	liang	ling	
z										
c										
s										
zh										
ch										
sh										
r										
j	ji	jia	jiao	jie	jiu	jian	jin	jiang	jing	jiong
q	qi	qia	qiao	qie	qiu	qian	qin	qiang	qing	qiong
x	xi	xia	xiao	xie	xiu	xian	xin	xiang	xing	xiong
g										
k										
h										
o	yi	ya	yao	ye	you	yan	yin	yang	ying	yong

yùn / shēng	u	ua	uo	uai	uei	uan	un	uang	ueng	ü	üe	üan	ün
b	bu												
p	pu												
m	mu												
f	fu												
d	du		duo		dui	duan	dun						
t	tu		tuo		tui	tuan	tun						
n	nu		nuo			nuan				nü	nüe		
l	lu		luo			luan	lun			lü	lüe		
z	zu		zuo		zui	zuan	zun						
c	cu		cuo		cui	cuan	cun						
s	su		suo		sui	suan	sun						
zh	zhu	zhua	zhuo	zhuai	zhui	zhuan	zhun	zhuang					
ch	chu		chuo	chuai	chui	chuan	chun	chuang					
sh	shu	shua	shuo	shuai	shui	shuan	shun	shuang					
r	ru		ruo		rui	ruan	run						
j										ju	jue	juan	jun
q										qu	que	quan	qun
x										xu	xue	xuan	xun
g	gu	gua	guo	guai	gui	guan	gun	guang					
k	ku	kua	kuo	kuai	kui	kuan	kun	kuang					
h	hu	hua	huo	huai	hui	huan	hun	huang					
o	wu	wa	wo	wai	wei	wan	wen	wang	weng	yu	yue	yuan	yun

5.4 Components of Chinese Characters (3) 一

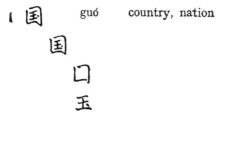

1 国   guó   country, nation

国

口

玉

2 汉字   hànzì   Chinese character

汉   字

氵   宀

又   子

Exercises

SIDE TWO

1) Read the Table of Chinese Phonetic Alphabet.

2) Practise reading the vowels and consonants:

a) Read aloud the vowels (according to the Table of the Chinese Vowels).

b) Read aloud the consonants several times according to the order of the position and manner of pronunciation as shown in the Table of the Chinese Consonants.

3) Read several times the Table of Compound Vowels and Vowels Plus Nasal Consonants.

4) Learn the Table of the Speech Sounds of Peking Dialect.

5) Pay attention to the basic strokes of the following components of Chinese characters and copy them.

1	口	丨 冂 口
2	玉	一 二 千 王 玉
3	氵	丶 冫 氵
4	又	𠃋 又
5	宀	丶 丷 宀
6	子	乛 了 子

Home Work

1) Review the Chinese vowels and consonants, and try to compare them with those of your own language.

2) Copy the alphabet (both the printed and the written).

3) Write the components of Chinese characters in this lesson five times.

Lesson 6

6.1 The Change of Tones

In the speech sounds of Peking dialect, the tones of syllables spoken in succession are different from those of the same syllables spoken separately. This difference is called the change of tones. The important rules of the change of tones are as follows:

(1) The neutral tone (or the light tone)

The four tones in the speech sounds of Peking dialect mentioned in the first two lessons, are the tones of stressed or accented syllables. In Chinese, when we read words separately, we always read it as a stressed syllable and therefore every word is given its own tone. In speaking, when a word is unstressed, it loses its original tone and becomes weak and short, that is to say, it becomes light in tone. For the convenience of teaching, the neutral tone is represented by the sign "₀" in writing. Strictly speaking, the neutral tone is much varied in pitch. The pitch of the neutral tone of a syllable is decided by the tone of the syllable preceding it and not by its original tone. The general rules are as follows:

After the 1st tone, the neutral tone is a semi-low light tone (2nd degree). e. g.

tādê　他的　(his)　　　　　ㄱ .|

After the 2nd tone, it is a middle light tone (3rd degree) e. g.

shéidê　誰的　(whose)　　ㄱ ·|

After the 3rd tone, it is a semi-high light tone (4th degree). e. g.

nǐdê　你的　(your)　　　　ㄴ ·|

After the 4th tone, it is a low light tone (1st degree). e. g.

dàdě 大的 (big one) ＼ .｜

(2) A syllable of the 3rd tone followed by a syllable of the 1st, 2nd, 4th, or neutral tone is pronounced only with a falling tone without its final rising, that is, its pitch becomes 21 (↘).* We call this falling tone the half-third tone. e. g.

3 + 1 ↘┐ ⟶ ↘┐ xiǎoshuō 小說
(novel)

3 + 2 ↘⁄ ⟶ ↘⁄ zǔguó 祖国
(fatherland)

3 + 4 ↘＼ ⟶ ↘＼ qǐngzuò 請坐
(Please, sit down.)

3 + 0 ↘ ·｜⟶ ↘ ·｜ xǐhuǎn 喜欢
(like, fond of)

(3) When a third tone is followed by another third tone, then the first third tone becomes a second tone (it is still marked in the third tone in writing). e. g.

3 + 3 ↘↘ ⟶ ⁄↘ hěnlěng 很冷
(very cold)

(4) When a third tone is followed by another third tone which has become a neutral tone, the first third tone is pronounced sometimes in the second tone and sometimes in the half-third tone. e. g.

3 + 0 ↘ ·｜ ⟶ ⁄ ·｜ lǎoshǔ 老鼠
(rat)

3 + 0 ↘ ·｜ ⟶ ↘ ·｜ jiějiě 姐姐
(elder sister)

(5) When a fourth tone is followed by another fourth tone, the first one does not fall so low as the 2nd one, they are pronounced as 53 51.† e. g.

4 + 4 ＼＼ ⟶ ＼＼ zàijiàn 再見
(Goodbye.)

---

* That is, from level 2 to level 1.

† That is, the first one falls only to level 3, the second one all the way to level 1.

6.2 Components of Chinese Characters (4)

1   你們   nǐmên   you

2   油   yóu   oil

3   只   zhǐ   only

Exercises
SIDE THREE, BAND ONE

1) Practise reading the following neutral tones:
   (to be read across)

chūqů	zhūzǐ	māmǎ	bāngzhǔ
láilê	xínglê	shénmô	péngyǒu
míngzǐ	dǒnglê	mǎibå	shàngwů
xièxiê	dìfâng	wànglê	kèqǐ

2) Practise reading the half-third tones:
   (to be read across)

Běijīng	huǒchē	hǎijūn	zhǐhuī
zǔguó	zhǔxí	jiǎnchá	xuǎnzé
zhǔyì	jiěfàng	gǎnxiè	lǐngxiù
běnzǐ	lǐzǐ	xǐhuân	

3) Practise reading the third tones followed by other third tones: (to be read across)

biǎoyǎn   zhǎnlǎn   shǒubiǎo
xuǎnjǔ   yǐngxiǎng

4) Practise reading the third tones followed by light tones (which are originally third tones):

xiǎngxiǎng   kěyî   nǎinâi   yǐzî

5) Practise reading the 4th tones followed by other 4th tones: (to be read across)

shìjiè   wànsuì   sùshè
yùndòng   zhùyì   zhèngzhì

6) Distinguish the following difficult sounds (1):

(1) b, p

bǎo	飽	full, to eat one's fill
pǎo	跑	to run
bǎolê	飽了	already full
pǎolê	跑了	to have run away
bēi	背	to carry on one's back
pēi	披	to put over one's shoulders
bēizhê	背着	carrying on one's back
pēizhê	披着	putting over one's shoulders

(2) d, t

dīng	釘	to nail, a nail
tīng	听	to listen, to hear
wǒdīng	我釘	I nail.
wǒtīng	我听	I listen.
dǎng	擋	to cover, to stand in one's way
tǎng	躺	to lie
dǎngzhê	擋着	covering, standing in one's way
tǎngzhê	躺着	lying

(3) g, k

gàn	干	to do
kàn	看	to see, to look at
gànwán	干完	to have done, finished
kànwán	看完	to have read through

ſ gōng	宮	palace
ι kōng	空	vacancy
ſ tiāngōng	天宮	celestial palace
ι tiānkōng	天空	sky, heaven

(4) zh, ch

ſ zhú	竹	bamboo
ι chú	厨	kitchen
ſ zhúzì	竹子	bamboo
ι chúzì	厨子	cook
ſ zhǔn	准	exact, punctual
ι chǔn	蠢	awkward, stupid
ſ zhēnzhǔn	真准	really exact, punctual
ι zhēnchǔn	真蠢	really awkward

(5) j, q

ſ jī	鷄	chicken
ι qī	漆	lacquer, to lacquer
ſ yóujī	油鷄	kind of chicken
ι yóuqī	油漆	lacquer, resinous varnish
ſ juàn	倦	tired
ι quàn	劝	to persuade, to advise
ſ bújuàn	不倦	not tired
ι búquàn	不劝	not to persuade or advise

(6) q, x

ſ qíng	晴	fine, clear
ι xíng	行	to walk, all right
ſ qínglė	晴了	to have cleared up
ι xínglė	行了	that will do, that is right

(7) j, x

ſ jù	剧	play
ι xù	序	order, preface
ſ jùmù	剧目	program
ι xùmù	序幕	prelude

7) Notice the basic strokes of the components of Chinese characters in this lesson and copy them.

1	亻	ノ 亻					
2	尔	㇄ (ノ ㇄)					
		小 (亅 ⺁ 小)					
3	門	丨 厂 卩 𠃌 𠃌 門 門 門
4	由	丶 冂 日 𢎘 由			
5	八	ノ 八					

Home Work

1) Read the exercises in this lesson several times, and pay special attention to the following:

 1) The second tone followed by the light tone;

 2) The pitch of the half-third tone;

 3) The difference between the aspirated sounds and the unaspirated sounds.

2) Copy the components of Chinese characters in this lesson five times,

Lesson 7

7.1 Summary on Tones

(1) The four tones:

ā	á	ǎ	à
zhē	zhé	zhě	zhè
jū	jú	jǔ	jù
qīng	qíng	qǐng	qìng
chōng	chóng	chǒng	chòng

(2) Neutral tones (light tones):

jīntiȧn	今天	(to-day)
míngtiȧn	明天	(to-morrow)
wǎnlė	晚了	(late)
dìfȧng	地方	(place)

(3) Changes of the 3rd tone:

3 + 1	⌄⌐→⌄⌐	shǒudū	首都	(capital)
3 + 2	⌄⌁→⌄⌁	zhěngqí	整齐	(tidiness)
3 + 3	⌄⌄→⌁⌄	jiǎngyǎn	讲演	(to give a speech)
3 + 4	⌄↘→⌄↘	lǐngxiù	领袖	(leader)
3 + 0	⌄·⌐→⌄·⌐	wǎnshȧng	晚上	(night)
3 + 0	⌄·⌐→⌁·⌐	děngdȩng	等等	(wait for a while)

(4) The pronunciation of two successive 4th tones:

4 + 4   ↘↘ ⟶ ↘↘   wànsuì   万岁   (Long live...)

7.2 Tones Deserving Special Attention

(1) Light tones:

míngtiȧn	wánlė	chúzi
shéiyȧ	wǒmȩn	dǒnglė
děngdȩng	kěyi	yǎnjing

shìdé xièxié zhùzì

duìlé

(2) 2nd tones plus 1st tones:

hóngjūn guójiā chénggōng Nánjīng

(3) 2nd tones plus 2nd tones:

rénmín hépíng wénxué yínháng

(4) 4th tones plus 2nd tones:

Lièníng èwén zhìfú liànxí

7.3 Discrimination of Tones

Shānxī	山西	(Shansi)
Shǎnxī	陝西	(Shensi)
zhǔyì	主义	(doctrine)
zhùyì	注意	(notice)
nǔlì	努力	(endeavor, effort)
núlì	奴隶	(slave)
yànhuì	宴会	(banquet)
yānhuī	烟灰	(ashes, soot)
dǒnglé	懂了	(to have understood)
dònglé	冻了	(frozen)
zhòngshì	重视	(to attach importance to, to deem highly)
zhōngshí	忠实	(faithful, loyal)
zhīyuán	支援	(to aid, to give support to)
zhìyuàn	志願	(voluntary)
yǎnjīng	眼睛	(eye)
yǎnjìng	眼鏡	(eye-glasses)
zhèngzhí	正直	(upright, righteous)
zhēngzhí	爭执	(dispute)
zhèngzhì	政治	(politics)
tōngzhī	通知	(to notify, to inform)
tóngzhì	同志	(comrade)
tǒngzhì	统治	(control)
shíyàn	实驗	(experiment)
shíyán	食盐	(salt)
shìyàn	試驗	(test)
shìyǎn	試演	(rehearsal)
shìyán	誓言	(oath, pledge)

7.4 Components of Chinese Characters (5)

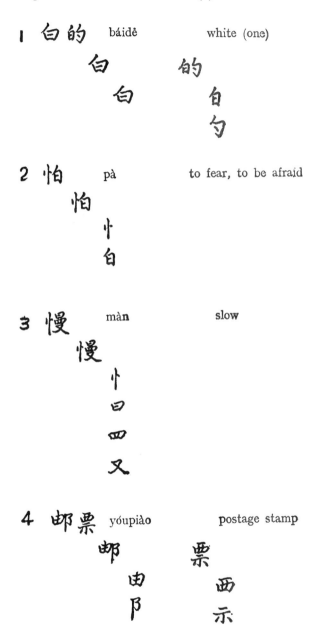

1 白的   báidê   white (one)

2 怕   pà   to fear, to be afraid

3 慢   màn   slow

4 邮票   yóupiào   postage stamp

Exercises
SIDE THREE, BAND TWO

1) Read the following four tones: (to be read across)

pāng	páng	pǎng	pàng
pīn	pín	pǐn	pìn
tān	tán	tǎn	tàn
kē	ké	kě	kè
zhōu	zhóu	zhǒu	zhòu
chēng	chéng	chěng	chèng
shē	shé	shě	shè
qiāng	qiáng	qiǎng	qiàng

Zhōngguójiěfàng
jīngshénkěpèi
shēnghuógǎishàn
fēichánggǎnxiè

2) Read the 2nd section of this lesson several times.
(to be read across)

3) Read the 3rd section of this lesson several times (Discrimination of tones).

4) Notice the basic strokes of the components of Chinese characters in this lesson and copy them.

1	白	ノ イ 台 白 白
2	勺	ノ 勺 勺
3	忄	丶 忄 忄
4	四	丶 冂 冂 四 四
5	阝	⁊ 弓 阝
6	西	一 冂 冃 西 西 西
7	示	一 二 示 ．

Home Work

1) Read the text and exercises in this lesson as many times as you can, paying special attention to the 2nd and 3rd sections.

2) Copy the components of the Chinese characters in this lesson five times.

Lesson 8

8.1 The Retroflex Ending "-r"

In Chinese, there are many words at the end of which the vowels are pronounced with the retroflex "r" Such vowels are called retroflex vowels, for the retroflex "r" and the vowel coming before it have been combined into one syllable. Some retroflex vowels are formed by adding the retroflex "r" to the vowels, and some are formed by dropping the final vowels or consonants out of words, and then adding the retroflex "r" to the main vowels. But in writing, only "r" is put after the original syllable.

(1) With "-r" added:

(a) "-a", "-o", "-e", "-u": "-r" is added directly. e. g.

xìfǎr (xìfǎr)	戏法兒	(trick, stunt)
gēr (gēr)	歌兒	(song)
cuòr (cuòr)	錯兒	(mistake)
xiǎotùr (xiǎotùr)	小兎兒	(little rabbit)

(b) "-ai", "-ei", "-an", "-en": "-r" is added after the final vowels or consonants have been dropped. e. g.

gàir (gàr)	盖兒	(cover)
wèir (wèr)	味兒	(smell)
pángbiānr (pángbiār)	旁边兒	(edge, margin, side)
fēnr (fēr)	分兒	(mark, work-unit)

(c) "-ng": The vowel before "-ng" must be nasalized, and is pronounced with the retroflex "r" (that is, in pronunciation, the breath is let out of the mouth and the nasal cavity at the same time). Here for the convenience of writing, "ng" is used as a symbol representing the nasalized element. e. g.

dànhuángr (dànhuángr)	蛋黃兒	(the yolk of an egg)
bǎndèngr (bǎndèngr)	板凳兒	(stool)

(2) With "er" added:

(a) "-i", "-ü": "er" is added after "-i" "-ü". e. g.

xiǎojīr (xiǎojiēr)　　　小鷄兒　(chicken)
xiǎoyúr (xiǎoyuér)　　　小魚兒　(little fish)

(b) "-in": "er" is added after the final consonant has been dropped. e. g.

xìnr (xièr)　　　　信兒　　(message)

(c) "-i": "i" after "zh", "ch", "sh", "r", "z", "c", "s" is changed into "er". e. g.

shìr (shèr)　　　　事兒　　(matter, business)

8.2 Polysyllables

(1) Dissyllables:

fēijī	飞机	(aeroplane)
Sūlián	苏联	(The Soviet Union)
yīngyǒng	英勇	(valiant)
yīyuàn	医院	(hospital)
nóngcūn	农村	(village)
wénxué	文学	(literature)
niúnǎi	牛奶	(milk)
shídài	时代	(times)
Běijīng	北京	(Peking)
zhǔxí	主席	(chairman)
zǒngtǒng	总统	(president)
jiěfàng	解放	(liberation)
yònggōng	用功	(studious)
dàxué	大学	(university)
zhèngfǔ	政府	(government)
jìhuà	計划	(plan)

(2) Trisyllables:

gòngqīngtuán	共青团	(The Communist Youth League)
hézuòshè	合作社	(co-operative store)
bówùyuàn	博物院	(museum)

(3) Four syllables:

chíjiǔhépíng	持久和平	(lasting peace)
guānliáozhǔyì	官僚主义	(bureaucracy)
xīnwénjìzhě	新闻記者	(journalist)

8.3 Components of Chinese Characters (6)

1 分兒   fēnr   mark, work-unit

分   兒
八   白
刀   儿

2 画兒   huàr   drawing, picture

画   兒
一   白
田   儿,
凵

3 快   kuài   quick. fast

快
忄
夬

4 放   fàng   to put

放
方
攵

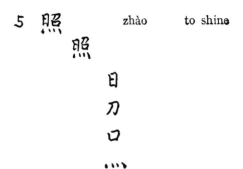

5   照   zhào   to shine

Exercises
SIDE THREE, BAND THREE

1) Practise the following retroflex vowels: (to be read down)

wánr	yíkuàir
biānr	gāngbǐtóur
zhèr	liànxíběnr
nàr	{ hǎohāorde
mòshuǐr	{ mànmānrde
shíhòur	

2) Distinguish the following difficult sounds (2):

(1) o, e

{ luò	落	(to fall)
{ lè	乐	(to laugh, glad)
{ luòle	落了	(to have fallen)
{ lèle	乐了	(to have laughed, to have been glad)
{ duó	夺	(to take by force)
{ dé	得	(to get)
{ duódào	夺到	(to have taken by force)
{ dédào	得到	(to have got)

(2) an, en

{ pán	盘	(plate)
{ pén	盆	(basin)
{ pánzi	盘子	(plate)
{ pénzi	盆子	(basin)

zhān	沾	(to soil)
zhēn	眞	(really, real)
zhāndê	沾的	(soiled)
zhēndê	眞的	(real, genuine)

(3) ang, eng

bàng	磅	(pound, to weigh)
bèng	蹦	(to hop, to jump)
bàngyíbàng	磅一磅	(to weigh once or for a little while)
bèngyíbèng	蹦一蹦	(to jump once or for a little while)
fāng	方	(square)
fēng	風	(wind)
dōngfāng	东方	(the east)
dōngfēng	东風	(east wind)

(4) an, ang

mán	蛮	(wild, barbaric)
máng	忙	(busy)
mánjílê	蛮極了	(extremely wild)
mángjílê	忙極了	(extremely busy)
tān	貪	(greed)
tāng	湯	(soup)
tānduō	貪多	(greedy)
tāngduō	湯多	(much soup)

(5) en, eng

fén	粉	(powder)
féng	諷	(to ridicule)
féncì	粉刺	(pimple)
féngcì	諷刺	(to ridicule, ridicule)
shēn	深	(deep)
shēng	生	(to give birth to, strange)
shēnshuǐ	深水	(deep water)
shēngshuǐ	生水	(unboiled water)

(6) s, sh

sì	四	(four)
shí	十	(ten)
sìshí	四十	(forty)
shísì	十四	(fourteen)

⎧ sān	三	(three)
⎩ shān	山	(hill)
⎧ sānlǐ	三里	(three ''li'')
⎩ shānlǐ	山里	(among the hills)

(7) z, c

⎧ zuò	作	(to do)
⎩ cuò	錯	(mistaken)
⎧ méizuò	沒作	(did not do)
⎩ méicuò	沒錯	(not mistaken)
⎧ zǎor	棗兒	(dates)
⎩ cǎor	草兒	(grass)
⎧ xiǎozǎor	小棗兒	(little dates)
⎩ xiǎocǎor	小草兒	(little grass)

(8) c, s

⎧ cì	刺	(to sting)
⎩ sì	寺	(abbey)
⎧ yígècì	一个刺	(one sting)
⎩ yígèsì	一个寺	(one abbey)
⎧ cāi	猜	(to guess)
⎩ sāi	塞	(to stop, to fill up)
⎧ cāiyicāi	猜一猜	(to make a guess)
⎩ sāiyìsāi	塞一塞	(to stop)

(9) i, ü

⎧ yìjiàn	意見	(opinion)
⎩ yùjiàn	遇見	(to meet)
⎧ méiyǒuyìjiàn	沒有意見	(no opinion)
⎩ méiyǒuyùjiàn	沒有遇見	(did not meet)
⎧ qī	期	(period)
⎩ qū	曲	(curved)
⎧ qīxiàn	期限	(limit of time)
⎩ qūxiàn	曲綫	(curve)

3) Pay attention to the basic strokes of the following components of Chinese characters and copy them.

1	八	丿 八
2	刀	刁 刀
3	白	丿 亻 仨 仴 伯 白
4	儿	丿 儿
5	田	丨 冂 冃 田 田
6	凵	乚 凵
7	夬	乛 ユ 尹 夬
8	方	丶 亠 亇 方
9	夂	丿 𠂇 夂 夂
10	灬	丶 丶丶 丶丶丶 丶丶丶丶

Home Work

1) Read correctly the words or word groups containing retroflex vowels in the exercises of this lesson.

2) Read as many times as possible the difficult sounds in pairs in the exercises of this lesson.

3) Copy five times the components of Chinese characters in this lesson.

Oral Exercises

Lesson 9

Shēngcí 生詞 New Words

SIDE THREE, BAND FOUR

1.	nǐ	你	you
2.	hǎo	好	well, good
3.	qǐng	請	please
4.	jìn	进	to come in, to enter
5.	zuò	坐	to sit (down)
6.	xièxiè	謝謝	thanks
7.	shì	是	to be
8.	něi	哪	which
9.	guó	国	country
10.	rén	人	person, man
11.	wǒ	我	I, me
12.	Yīngguó	英国	Great Britain
13.	huì	会	can
14.	shuō	说	to speak, to say
15.	zhōngwén	中文	the Chinese language
16.	mā	嗎	(an interrogative particle)
17.	bù	不	not, no
18.	yīngwén	英文	English
19.	tā	他	he, him
20.	Zhōngguó	中国	China
21.	jiào	叫	to call, to be called
22.	shénmǒ	什么	what
23.	míngzì	名字	name

Duǎnjù 短句 Simple Sentences

SIDE THREE, BAND FOUR

(1) Nǐ   hǎo!

你 好!

How are you?

(2) Nǐ   hǎo.

你 好!

How are you?

(3) Qǐng   jìn!

請 进!

Come in, please.

(4) Qǐng   zuò!

請 坐!

Sit down, please!

(5) Xièxiè.

謝謝.

Thanks.

(6) Nǐ   shì   něiguó   rén?

你 是 哪国 人?

Where do you come from?

(7) Wǒ   shì   Yīngguó   rén.

我 是 英国 人.

I am an Englishman.

(8) Nǐ   huì   shuō   zhōngwén   mā?

你 会 说 中文 吗?

Do you speak Chinese?

(9) Bú   huì,   wǒ   shuō   yīngwén.

不 会, 我 说 英文.

No, I speak English.

(10) Tā   shì   něiguó   rén?

他 是 哪国 人?

Where does he come from?

(11) Tā   shì   Zhōngguó   rén.

他 是 中国 人.

He is Chinese.

(12) Nǐ   jiào   shénmó   míngzì?

你 叫 什么 名字?

What is your name?

(13) Wǒ   jiào ——.

我 叫 ——.

My name is——.

(14) Tā jiào shénmő míngzì?
他 叫 什么 名字？   What is his name?

(15) Tā jiào ——.
他 叫 ——.   His name is____.

Hànzì zìsù 汉字字素
Components of Chinese Characters

1 好   hǎo   good, well

好

女
子

2 請进   qǐngjìn   Come in, please.

請   进

言   井
青   辶

3 是   shì   yes, to be

是

日
疋

4 次   cì   time

次

冫
欠

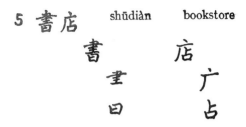

5 書店　　shūdiàn　　bookstore

Jīběn bǐhuà　　基本笔划
Basic Strokes

1	女	ノ く 女 女
2	言	、 ー 亠 亖 言
3	青	ー 二 キ 主 青 青 青 青
4	井	ー 二 キ 井
5	辶	、 氵 辶
6	疋	ー 丁 下 下 疋 疋
7	ン	、 ン
8	欠	⌒ ク 欠 ⺈
9	聿	⊐ ⊐ ⊐ 肀 肀 聿
10	广	、 亠 广
11	占	丨 卜 占

Lesson 10

Shēngcí 生詞 New Words

1.	shéi	誰	who
2.	xuéshēng	学生	student
3.	xiānshēng	先生	teacher
4.	yǒu	有	to have, there is (are)
5.	kè	課	lesson, class
6.	méiyǒu	沒有	to have no..., to have none, not to have...
7.	xiàwǔ	下午	afternoon
8.	fǔdǎo	輔导	to help...to study
9.	zài	在	at, in, on
10.	nǎr	哪兒	where
11.	wǒmēndè	我們的	our, ours
12.	jiàoshǐ	教室	classroom
13.	jǐ	几	how many
14.	diǎnzhōng	点鐘	hour
15.	kāishǐ	开始	to begin, to start
16.	sāndiǎn	三点	three o'clock
17.	bàn	半	half
18.	xuéxí	学習	to learn
19.	Běidà	北大	Peking University
20.	yě	也	also, too

Duǎnjù 短句 Simple Sentences

SIDE FOUR, BAND ONE

(1) Tā shì shéi?

他 是 誰?

Who is he?

(2) Tā shì xuéshēng.

他 是 学生.

He is a student.

(3) Tā shì shéi?

他 是 誰?

Who is he?

(4) Tā shì xiānshēng.

他 是 先生.

He is a teacher.

(5) Nǐ yǒu kè må?

你 有 課 嗎?

Do you have classes?

(6) Yǒu kè.

有 課.

I do.

(7) Méi yǒu.

沒 有.

I don't.

(8) Nǐ xiàwǔ yǒu kè må?

你 下午 有 課 嗎?

Do you have classes in the afternoon?

(9) Méi yǒu kè, yǒu fǔdǎo.

沒 有 課, 有 輔导.

I don't, but my teacher will come to help me study.

(10) Zài nǎr fǔdǎo?

在 哪兒 輔导?

Where will your teacher come to help you?

(11) Zài wǒmêndê jiàoshǐ.

在 我們的 教室.

In our classroom.

(12) Jǐ diǎnzhōng kāishǐ fǔdǎo?

几 点鐘 开始 輔导?

When will your teacher come to help you?

(13) Sāndiǎn bàn.

三点 半.

Half past three.

(14) Nǐ zài nǎr xuéxí?

你 在 哪兒 学習?

Where are you studying?

(15) Wǒ　zài　Běidà　xuéxí.

我 在 北大 学習.　I am studying in Peking University.

(16) Tā　zài　nǎr　xuéxí?

他 在 哪兒 学習?　Where is he studying?

(17) Tā yě zài Běidà xuéxí.

他也在北大学習.　He is also studying in Peking University.

Hànzì zìsù　汉字字素
Components of Chinese Characters

1 誰　　　shéi　　　who

　　誰
　　言
　　隹

2 沿　　　yán　　　along

　　沿
　　氵
　　几
　　口

3 疼　　　téng　　　painful

　　疼
　　疒
　　夂
　　冫

4 新的   xīndê   new (one)

新   的

立
木
斤

白
勺

5 草   cǎo   grass

草

屮
日
十

6 外边   wàibiân   outside

外

夕
卜

边

力
辶

Jīběn bǐhuà   基本笔划
Basic Strokes

1	佳	亻 亻 亻 亻 亻 佳 佳
2	几	丿 几
3	疒	广 疒
4	夂	丿 夂 夂
5	立	丶 二 亠 亠 立
6	木	一 十 才 木
7	斤	丿 亻 斤 斤
8	业	丨 业 业 业
9	十	一 十
10	夕	丿 夕 夕
11	卜	丨 卜
12	力	乛 力

Lesson 11

Shēngcí 生詞 New Words

SIDE FOUR, BAND TWO

1.	shàngkè	上課	to have classes, to go to classes
2.	lē	了	(a modal particle)
3.	hái	还	still, yet
4.	nē	呢	(a modal particle)
5.	wèntí	問題	question, problem
6.	dǒnglē	懂了	to have understood
7.	duìlē	对了	right
8.	nán	难	difficult
9.	dàshēng	大声	loudly, aloud
10.	zài	再	again, once more
11.	niàn	念	to read
12.	yíbiàn	一遍	one time, once
13.	xiě	写	to write
14.	dàjiā	大家	all (the people)
15.	yíkuàir	一塊兒	together
16.	gēn	跟	with, after, to follow
17.	tīng	听	to hear, to listen
18.	wèn	問	to ask, to inquire
19.	huídá	回答	to answer

20. xiàkè 下課 the class is over, after class
21. zàijiàn 再見 good-bye

Duǎnjù 短句 Simple Sentences

SIDE FOUR, BAND TWO

(1) Shàng kè lê mâ?
上 課 了 嗎? Is it time for class?

(2) Shàng kè lê.
上 課 了. It is.

(3) Hái méi yǒu nê!
还 沒 有 呢! Not yet.

(4) Nǐ yǒu wèntí mâ?
你 有 問題 嗎? Have you any question?

(5) Yǒu.
有. Yes, I have.

(6) Méi yǒu.
沒 有. No, I have none.

(7) Nǐ dǒng lê mâ?
你 懂 了 嗎? Do you understand?

(8) Dǒng lê.
懂 了. I do.

(9) Bù dǒng.
不 懂. I don't.

(10) Duì lê mâ?
对 了 嗎? Is it right?

(11) Duì lê.
对 了. It is right.

(12) Bú duì.
不 对. No, it isn't.

(13) Nán bù nán?
难 不 难? Is it difficult?

(14) Nán.
难. It is.

(15) Bù nán.
不 难. No, it isn't.

(16) Qǐng nǐ niàn.
请 你 念. Please read.

(17) Qǐng nǐ dà shēng niàn.
請 你 大 声 念. Please read loudly.

(18) Qǐng nǐ zài niàn yíbiàn.
請 你 再 念 一 遍. Please read it once more.

(19) Qǐng nǐ xiě.
請 你 写. Please write.

(20) Qǐng nǐ zài xiě yíbiàn.
請 你 再 写 一 遍. Please write it once more.

(21) Dàjiā yíkuàir niàn.
大家 一塊兒 念. All of you read together.

(22) Dàjiā gēn wǒ niàn.
大家 跟 我 念. All of you read after me.

(23) Wǒ niàn, nǐmen tīng.
我 念, 你們 听. I'll read, and will you please listen.

(24) Wǒ shuō, nǐmen xiě.
我 說, 你們 写. I'll speak, and will you please write it down.

(25) Wǒ wèn, nǐmen huídá.
我 問, 你們 回答. I'll ask and you'll answer.

(26) Hǎo, xià kè le, zàijiàn!
好, 下 課 了, 再見! All right, class is over, good-bye!

(27) Zàijiàn!
再見! Good-bye!

Hànzì zìsù   汉字字素

Components of Chinese Characters

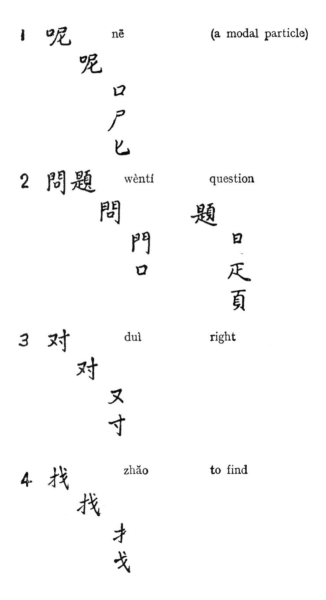

1   呢   nē   (a modal particle)

呢

口

尸

匕

2   問題   wèntí   question

問   題

門   日

口   疋

頁

3   对   duì   right

对

又

寸

4   找   zhǎo   to find

找

扌

戈

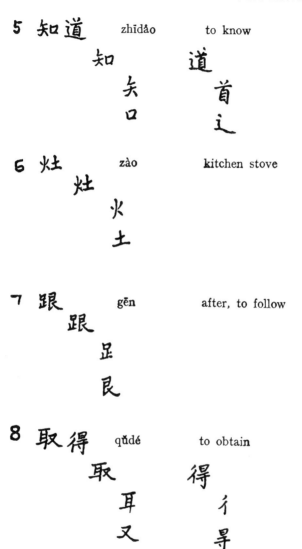

5 知道   zhīdào   to know

知   道
    矢   首
    口   辶

6 灶   zào   kitchen stove

灶
    火
    土

7 跟   gēn   after, to follow

跟
    𧾷
    艮

8 取得   qǔdé   to obtain

取   得
    耳   彳
    又   寻

Jīběn bǐhuà 基本笔划
Basic Strokes

1	尸	⁊ ⁊ 尸
2	匕	ノ 匕
3	頁	一 丆 厂 万 百 百 頁
4	寸	一 寸 寸
5	才	一 十 才
6	戈	一 弋 戈 戈
7	矢	ノ ㇉ 匕 午 矢
8	首	丶 丷 丷 ⺍ 产 首 首 首
9	火	丶 ⺈ ⺀ 火
10	足	口 ‷ ‷ ⻊ 足
11	艮	⁊ ⁊ ヨ 艮 艮 艮
12	耳	一 丆 Ⅱ 丌 耳 耳
13	彳	ノ ㇒ 彳
14	尋	口 旦 尋

Lesson 12

Shēngcí 生詞 New Words

SIDE FOUR, BAND THREE

1.	tóngzhì	同志	comrade
2.	dào	到	to go (to), to arrive
3.	qù	去	to go
4.	shítáng	食堂	dining hall, refectory
5.	túshūguǎn	圖書館	library
6.	hézuòshè	合作社	co-operative store
7.	yào	要	to want
8.	mǎi	买	to buy
9.	dōngxi	东西	thing
10.	běnzi	本子	note-book
11.	qiānbǐ	鉛笔	pencil
12.	shū	書	book
13.	hé	和	and
14.	zhǐ	紙	paper
15.	duōshǎo	多少	how many, how much
16.	qián	錢	money
17.	liǎng	两	two
18.	máo	毛	ten cents
19.	wǔ	五	five
20.	yī	一	one
21.	kuài	块	dollar (a measure word)
22.	jìnchéng	进城	to go to the city
23.	sùshè	宿舍	dormitory

24. xiànzài   現在   now
25. huí   回   to return

Duǎnjù 短句 Simple Sentences

SIDE FOUR, BAND THREE

(1) Tóngzhì! nǐ dào nǎr qù?
同志! 你 到 哪兒 去?
Comrade! Where are you going?

(2) Wǒ dào shítáng qù.
我 到 食堂 去.
I am going to the dining hall.

(3) Wǒ huí sùshè qù.
我 回 宿舍 去.
I am returning to the dormitory.

(4) Tā dào nǎr qù?
他 到 哪兒 去?
Where is he going?

(5) Tā dào túshūguǎn qù.
他 到 圖書館 去.
He is going to the library.

(6) Nǐ qù hézuòshè mǎ?
你 去 合作社 嗎?
Are you going to the co-operative store?

(7) Qù.
去.
Yes, I am.

(8) Bú qù.
不 去.
No, I am not.

(9) Nǐ yào mǎi shénmǒ dōngxi?
你 要 买 什么 东西?
What do you want to buy?

(10) Wǒ yào mǎi běnzi.
我 要 买 本子.
I want to buy note-books.

(11) Wǒ yào mǎi qiānbǐ.
我 要 买 鉛笔.
I want to buy pencils.

(12) Tā yào mǎi shénmǒ dōngxi?
他 要 买 什么 东西?
What does he want to buy?

(13) Tā yào mǎi shū hé zhǐ.
他 要 买 書 和 纸.
He wants to buy books and paper.

(14) Běnzi   duōshǎo   qián?

本子　多少　錢？

How much is the note-book?

(15) Liǎngmáo wǔ.

两毛　五.

Twenty-five cents.

(16) Shū   duōshǎo   qián?

書　多少　錢？

How much is the book?

(17) Yíkuài   qián.

一塊　錢.

One dollar.

(18) Nǐ xiànzài jìn chéng må?

你现在进城嗎？

Are you going to the city now?

(19) Jìn   chéng.

进　城.

Yes, I am going to the city.

(20) Bú   jìn   chéng.

不　进　城.

No, I am not going to the city.

Hànzì zìsù 汉字字素

Components of Chinese Characters

3　飯　　fàn　　　　　　meal

飯
食
反

4　合作社　　hézuòshè　　co-operative store

合　　　作　　　　社
人　　　亻　　　　　礻
一　　　乍　　　　　土
口

5　袖子　　xiùzǐ　　　　sleeve

袖　　子
礻　　子
由

6　鉛笔　　qiānbǐ　　　pencil

鉛　　　笔
金　　　竹
几　　　毛
口

7　紙　　zhǐ　　　paper

紙
糸
氏

8 雷 léi thunder

雷

雨
田

Jīběn bǐhuà 基本笔划
Basic Strokes

1	冂	丨 冂
2	士	十 士
3	心	丶 心 心 心
4	刂	丨 刂
5	食	丿 丶 ト 彑 亽 倉 食 食
6	反	丿 厂 反
7	人	丿 人
8	乍	丿 亡 仁 乍 乍
9	礻	丶 亅 才 礻
10	衤	衤 衤
11	金	人 丘 仐 仐 金 金
12	竹	丿 亡 仁 丬 竹 竹
13	毛	丿 仁 三 毛
14	糸	乚 幺 幺 糸 糸 糸
15	氏	丿 仁 匕 氏
16	雨	一 丆 丙 雨 雨 雨 雨 雨

Basic Grammar

Abbreviations Adopted in the Words Columns

(名)	名　詞 The Noun	Míngcí
(代)	代　詞 The Pronoun	Dàicí
(动)	动　詞 The Verb	Dòngcí
(能动)	能願动詞 The Optative Verb	néngyuàndòngcí
(数)	数　詞 The Numeral	Shùcí
(形)	形 容 詞 The Adjective	Xíngróngcí
(介)	介　詞 The Preposition	Jìecí
(副)	副　詞 The Adverb	Fùcí
(連)	連　詞 The Conjunction	Liáncí
(嘆)	嘆　詞 The Interjection	Tàncí
(助)	助　詞 The Particle	Zhùcí
(头)	詞　头 The Prefix	Cítóu
(尾)	詞　尾 The Suffix	Cíwěi

Lesson 13

生詞 Shēngcí New Words
SIDE FOUR, BAND FOUR

1.	这	(代) zhèi, zhè	this
2.	是	(动) shì	to be
3.	書	(名) shū	book
4.	我	(代) wǒ	I, me
5.	学生	(名) xuéshēng	student
6.	先生	(名) xiānshēng	teacher, Mr, sir
7.	中国	(名) Zhōngguó	China, Chinese
8.	人	(名) rén	man, person
9.	那	(代) nèi, nà	that
10.	不	(副) bù	not, no
11.	你	(代) nǐ	you
12.	嗎	(助) mā	(an interrogative particle)
13.	您	(代) nín	(the polite form of 你)
14.	报	(名) bào	newspaper
15.	他	(代) tā	he, him

語法 Yǔfǎ Grammar

13.1 The Sentence with a Substantive Predicate (1)   In modern Chinese, sentences may be divided into four kinds, according to the construction of the predicate. The first kind is the sentence with a substantive predicate. Here we will deal with the sentence with a substantive predicate (1).

A sentence, in which the main element of the predicate is made up of a substantive, is called the sentence with a substantive predicate (1). The substantive may be a noun, a pronoun, or a numeral; it tells "what" the person or thing is as required by the subject. The copula may be looked upon as a particular verb used to connect the subject with the substantive in the predicate. The predicate which is composed of a substantive and a copula must explain the subject. e. g.

1. 这　　是　　书.
   Zhèi　　shì　　shū.

   This is a book.

2. 我　　是　　学生.
   Wǒ　　shì　　xuéshēng.

   I am a student.

3. 先生　　是　　中国　　人.
   Xiānshēng　　shì　　Zhōngguó　　rén.

   The teacher is Chinese (LIT.: China person).

这, 我 , and 先生 are subjects; 是书, 是学生, and 是中国人 are predicates. All the words after the copula are nouns.

13.2 **The Negative Form of the Sentence with a Substantive Predicate (1)** The negative form of such kind of sentence is made by putting the negative adverb 不 before the copula 是. e. g.

4. 那　　不　　是　　书.
   Nèi　　bú　　shì　　shū.

   That is not a book.

5. 你　　不　　是　　先生.
   Nǐ　　bú　　shì　　xiānshēng.

   You are not a teacher.

6. 学生　　不　　是　　中国　　人.
Xuéshēng　bú　shì　Zhōngguó　rén.

The student is not Chinese.

The adverb 不 is pronounced in the 4th tone when it is used independently or followed by a syllable of the 1st, 2nd or 3rd tone; but it is pronounced in the 2nd tone when it is followed by a syllable of the 4th tone. Hence, in the above three examples, 不 is in the 2nd tone.

13.3 The Interrogative Sentence (1)   In modern Chinese, there are five kinds of interrogative sentences that are frequently used. Here, we will deal with the first kind. When we put the interrogative modal particle 吗 at the end of a declarative sentence (affirmative or negative), it is changed into an interrogative sentence. e. g.

7. 这　　是　　書　　吗?
Zhèi　shì　shū　mǎ?

Is this a book?

8. 这　　不　　是　　書　　吗?
Zhèi　bú　shì　shū　mǎ?

Isn't this a book?

13.4 你 and 您   你 and 您 are both in the second person singular. But 您 is a polite form, and used only when we wish to pay respect to the person in question. e. g.

9. 您　　不　　是　　学生,　　您　　是　　先生.
Nín　bú　shì　xuéshēng,　nín　shì　xiānshēng.

You (formal) are not a student, you are a teacher.

課文 Kèwén Text

SIDE FOUR, BAND FOUR

I

1. 这 是 書.
   Zhèi shì shū.
   This is a book.

2. 那 是 报.
   Nèi shì bào.
   That is a newspaper.

3. 他 是 先生.
   Tā shì xiānshěng.
   He is the (OR a) teacher.

4. 我 是 学生.
   Wǒ shì xuéshěng.
   I am a student.

5. 先生 是 中国 人.
   Xiānshěng shì Zhōngguó rén.
   The teacher is Chinese (LIT.: a China person).

II

6. 这 不 是 書.
   Zhèi bú shì shū.
   This is not a book.

7. 那 不 是 报.
   Nèi bú shì bào.
   That is not a newspaper.

8. 我 不 是 先生.
   Wǒ bú shì xiānshěng.
   I am not the teacher.

9. 您 不 是 学生.
   Nín bú shì xuéshěng.
   You (formal "you") are not a student.

10. 他　不　是　中国　人.
　　Tā　bú　shì　Zhōngguó　rén.
　　He is not Chinese.

III

11. 这　是　书，那　是　报.
　　Zhèi　shì　shū,　nèi　shì　bào.
　　This is a book, that is a newspaper.

12. 这　是　书，这　不　是　报.
　　Zhèi　shì　shū,　zhèi　bú　shì　bào.
　　This is a book, this is not a newspaper.

13. 那　不　是　报，那　是　书.
　　Nèi　bú　shì　bào,　nèi　shì　shū.
　　That is not a newspaper, that is a book.

14. 我　是　学生，您　是　先生.
　　Wǒ　shì　xuéshěng,　nín　shì　xiānshěng.
　　I am a student, you (formal) are the teacher.

15. 他　不　是　先生，他　是　学生.
　　Tā　bú　shì　xiānshěng,　tā　shì　xuéshěng.
　　He is not a teacher, he is a student.

IV

(a₁)　这　是　书　吗?
　　　Zhèi　shì　shū　mǎ?
　　　Is this a book?

(b₁)　这　是　书.
　　　Zhèi　shì　shū.
　　　This is a book. (= Yes.)

(a₂)　那　是　报　吗?
　　　Nèi　shì　bào　mǎ?
　　　Is that a newspaper?

(b₂) 那 不 是 报, 那 是 书.
Nèi bú shì bào, nèi shì shū.

That is not a newspaper, that is a book. (= No, that is a book.)

(a₃) 你 是 学生 吗?
Nǐ shì xuéshēng mǎ?

Are you a student?

(b₃) 我 是 学生.
Wǒ shì xuéshēng.

I am a student. (=Yes.)

(a₄) 他 是 中国 人 吗?
Tā shì Zhōngguó rén mǎ?

Is he Chinese?

(b₄) 他 不 是 中国 人.
Tā bú shì Zhōngguó rén.

He is not Chinese. (=No.)

课外练习 Kèwài liànxí Home Work

1) Copy all the new words once.

2) Transcribe the following sentences by using the phonetic alphabet and give the correct tone of each syllable:

(1) 我 是 学生.

(2) 他 不 是 先生.

(3) 这 是 书 吗?

3) Answer the following questions with Chinese characters:

(4) 你 是 中国 人 吗?

(5) 那 是 报 吗?

汉字表　Hànzì biǎo　Chinese Characters

1	这	文（丶 一 ナ 文 ）
		辶
2	是	
3	書	
4	我	丿 二 千 扌 找 我 我
5	学	兴（丶 丷 ⺍ ⺜ 兴 ）
		子
6	生	丿 ⺊ ⺌ 牛 生
7	先	丿 ⺊ ⺌ 生 先
8	中	丶 冂 口 中
9	国	
10	人	
11	那	月（刀 刃 月 ）
		阝
12	不	一 丆 万 不
13	你	
14	嗎	口
		馬（一 二 三 丰 丐 馬 馬 ）
15	您	你
		心

16	报	扌
		及（⁻ ⼫ 及）
17	他	亻
		也（⼂ ⼔ 也）

Lesson 14

生詞 Shēngcí New Words

SIDE FOUR, BAND FIVE

1.	一	(数) yī	a, one
2.	本	(量) běn	(a measure word)
3.	个	(量) gè	(a measure word)
4.	三	(数) sān	three
5.	很	(副) hěn	very
6.	新	(形) xīn	new
7.	好	(形) hǎo	good, well
8.	張	(量) zhāng	(a measure word)
9.	紙	(名) zhǐ [張]	paper
10.	小	(形) xiǎo	little, small
11.	大	(形) dà	big, large
12.	多	(形) duō	many, much
13.	少	(形) shǎo	few, little
14.	北京	(名) Běijīng	Peking
15.	旧	(形) jiù	old

語法 Yǔfǎ Grammar

14.1 The Nominal Measure Word Persons, things and actions may all be numbered or weighed. The words showing the numerical or quantitative units of persons or things, are called nominal measure words; and those. which indicate such units of actions are called verbal measure words. Here we will deal with the nominal measure words.

In modern Chinese, generally speaking, a numeral (such as 一) or a demonstrative pronoun (such as 这 and 那) cannot be directly used with a noun; a measure word should always be used between it and the noun. e. g.

1. 这　是　一本　书.
   Zhèi　shì　yìběn　shū.
   This is a (one) book.

2. 那个　学生　是　中国　人.
   Nèigě　xuéshěng　shì　Zhōngguó　rén.
   That student is Chinese.

We cannot say 一书 or 那学生, for after 一 and 那 there should be a measure word.

Many nouns have their specific measure words, for example, 本 is the specific measure word for 书. 个 is a very common measure word, and is most extensively used, for it may be used in connection with persons (e. g. the measure word of 学生 is 个.), and also in the case of things that have no specific measure words for themselves. It may even be substituted for other specific measure words.

The following four points should be observed in using measure words:

(1) When there are a demonstrative pronoun and a numeral before the measure word, the demonstrative pronoun should be put before the numeral. e. g.

3. 这　三个　学生
   zhèi　sāngě　xuéshěng
   these three students

4. 那　三本　书
   nèi　sānběn　shū
   those three books

(2) The measure word is directly annexed to the demonstrative pronoun or the numeral. e. g.

5. 这个　　学生
　　zhèigè　xuéshēng

　　this student

6. 三本　　书
　　sānběn　shū

　　three books

If there is no numeral or demonstrative pronoun, then no measure word can be allowed to stand alone before a noun. For instance, we can never say such a thing as 个先生是中国人.

(3) There are a few nouns which possess in themselves the nature or function of the measure word, and hence do not require measure words when they are preceded by numerals or demonstrative pronouns. e. g. 一年 (one year) and 这課 (this lesson).

(4) When the person or thing denoted by the noun is already clearly defined in the context, the noun after the measure word may be omitted. e. g.

7. 这个　　中国　　人　　是　　先生,
　　Zhèigè　Zhōngguó　rén　shì　xiānshēng,

　　那个　　(中国　　人)　　是　　学生.
　　nèigè　(Zhōngguó　rén)　shì　xuéshēng.

This Chinese is a teacher, that one (Chinese) is a student.

中国人 after 那个 may be omitted.

14.2 The Tones of 一 The tones of the numeral 一 vary:
(1) When it stands alone; or when reading a number of more than one figure, if one does not read the names of the decimal units, e. g. 1910 (一九一〇), 01521 (〇一五二一); or if 一 is the last figure of a number of more than one figure, e. g. 二十一 or 七百六十一, it is pronounced in the 1st tone.

(2) When it is followed by a syllable of the 1st, 2nd or 3rd tone, or by a syllable of the neutral tone that is originally in the 1st, 2nd or 3rd tone, it is pronounced in the 4th tone. e. g. yìzhāng zhǐ (a sheet of paper), yìtiáo lù (a way) and yìběn shū (a book).

(3) When it is followed by a syllable of the 4th tone, or by a syllable of the neutral tone that is originally in the 4th tone, it is pronounced in the 2nd tone. e. g. yígè rén (a person).

14.3 The Sentence with an Adjectival Predicate A sentence, of which the predicate is composed of an adjective, is called the sentence with an adjectival predicate. An adjective is a word used to show the quality or appearance of a person or thing. Therefore, in a sentence with an adjectival predicate, the predicate is used to describe the quality, appearance and so forth of the person or thing denoted by the subject. In other words, the predicate tells us chiefly "how" is the person or thing denoted by the subject. e. g.

8. 这本 书 很 新.
Zhèiběn shū hěn xīn.

This book is very new.

9. 那个 学生 很 好.
Nèigė xuéshêng hěn hǎo.

That student is very good.

书 and 学生 are subjects. 新 and 好 are predicates. In the predicates, 很 is an adverb of degree, used as adverbial modifier modifying the adjectives 新 and 好.

If we wish to negate a sentence with an adjectival predicate, we simply put the negative adverb 不 before the adjective. e. g.

10. 这本 书 不 好.
Zhèiběn shū bù hǎo.

This book is not good.

11. 那張 紙 不 小.
Nèizhāng zhǐ bù xiǎo.

That (sheet of) paper is not small.

There are two points worth noticing concerning the sentence with an adjectival predicate:

(1) Before the adjectival predicate, the copula 是 is never used. This is a characteristic of Chinese syntax.

(2) The adverb 很 is often used before a simple predicative adjective in an affirmative declarative sentence. In such a case, it is very weak, having completely lost its significance as a word emphasizing degree (but it is not so in negative and

interrogative sentences). An adjectival predicate without such an adverbial modifier implies a sense of comparison, for instance, when we say 这本書新 it implies also 那本書旧. Therefore, such expressions are often used in comparisons. e. g.

12. 这張　紙　大,　那張　紙　小.
Zhèizhāng zhǐ dà, nèizhāng zhǐ xiǎo.

This sheet of paper is big, that sheet of paper is small.

13. 这本　書　好,　那本　書　不　好.
Zhèiběn shū hǎo, nèiběn shū bù hǎo.

This book is good, that book is not good.

14.4 多 and 少 多 and 少, two very common adjectives, may also be used as predicates. In such a case, either of them may be used alone as a predicate (implying comparison), and be preceded by an adverbial modifier. e. g.

14. 学生　多,　先生　少.
Xuéshēng duō, xiānshēng shǎo.

The students are many, the teachers are few.

15. 学生　很　多.
Xuéshēng hěn duō.

There are (very) many students.

16. 先生　很　少.
Xiānshēng hěn shǎo.

There are (very) few teachers.

But as adjective modifiers of nouns, they are different from other adjectives: we must say 很多 or 很少, though the word 很 is rather weak in meaning. We cannot say 多先生是北京人, but we must say:

17. 很　多　先生　是　北京　人.
Hěn duō xiānshēng shì Běijīng rén.

(Very) many teachers come from Peking (LIT.: are Peking people).

課文 Kèwén Text

SIDE FOUR, BAND FIVE

I

1. 这 是 一本 書.
   Zhèi shì yìběn shū.

   This is a (one) book.

2. 这 是 一張 纸, 那 是 一張 报.
   Zhèi shì yìzhāng zhǐ, nèi shì yìzhāng bào.

   This is a sheet of paper, that is a (sheet of) newspaper.

3. 这張 纸 大, 那張 纸 小.
   Zhèizhāng zhǐ dà, nèizhāng zhǐ xiǎo.

   This sheet of paper is big, that one (that sheet of paper) is little.

II

4. 这 是 一本 書.
   Zhèi shì yìběn shū.

   This is a book.

5. 这本 書 很 新.
   Zhèiběn shū hěn xīn.

   This book is (very) new.

6. 这本 書 新, 那本 書 旧.
   Zhèiběn shū xīn, nèiběn shū jiù.

   This book is new, that book is old.

7. 这本 書 很 好.
   Zhèiběn shū hěn hǎo.

   This book is (very) good.

8. 这本　書　好，那本　書　不　好.
Zhèiběn　shū　hǎo,　nèiběn　shū　bù　hǎo.

This book is good, that book is not good.

III

9. 这　一个　中国　人　是　学生.
Zhèi　yígě　Zhōngguó　rén　shì　xuéshěng.

This (one) Chinese (person) is a student.

10. 这个　学生　很　好.
Zhèigě　xuéshěng　hěn　hǎo.

This student is (very) good.

11. 很　多　学生　是　北京　人.
Hěn　duō　xuéshěng　shì　Běijīng　rén.

Many students are from Peking (LIT.: are Peking people).

12. 那　一个　中国　人　是　先生.
Nèi　yígě　Zhōngguó　rén　shì　xiānshěng.

That Chinese is the (OR a) teacher.

13. 那个　先生　很　好.
Nèigě　xiānshěng　hěn　hǎo.

That teacher is (very) good.

14. 很　多　先生　是　北京　人.
Hěn　duō　xiānshěng　shì　Běijīng　rén.

Many teachers are from Peking.

IV

(a₁) 这　是　書　吗?
Zhèi　shì　shū　mǎ?

Is this a book?

(b₁) 这 不 是 书, 那 是 书.
Zhèi bú shì shū, nèi shì shū.
This is not a book, that is a book.

(a₂) 那本 书 好 吗?
Nèiběn shū hǎo må?
Is that book good?

(b₂) 那本 书 不 好, 这本 书 好.
Nèiběn shū bù hǎo, zhèiběn shū hǎo.
That book is not good, this book is good.

(a₃) 很 多 先生 是 北京 人 吗?
Hěn duō xiānshēng shì Běijīng rén må?
Are many teachers from Peking?

(b₃) 很 多 先生 是 北京 人.
Hěn duō xiānshēng shì Běijīng rén.
Many teachers are from Peking. (= Yes.)

(a₄) 很 多 学生 是 北京 人 吗?
Hěn duō xuéshēng shì Běijīng rén må?
Are many students from Peking?

(b₄) 很 多 学生 是 北京 人.
Hěn duō xuéshēng shì Běijīng rén.
Many students are from Peking. (= Yes.)

課外練習 Kèwài liànxí Home Work

1) Copy all the new words in this lesson once.

2) Change the following phonetic spellings into Chinese characters:

(1) Xuéshēng hěn duō.
(2) Bào hěn shǎo.

3) Copy and fill these blanks with proper measure words:

(3) 这 是 一___ 纸.

(4) 那＿＿＿　書　很　好.

(5) 那＿＿＿　学生　是　中国　人　嗎?

4) Translate and answer the following questions:

   (6) Is that sheet of paper big ?

   (7) Is that book old ?

   (8) Is this Chinese the new teacher ?

汉字表　Hànzì biǎo　Chinese Characters

1	一	
2	本	木 本
3	个	人 个
4	三	一 二 三
5	很	彳
		艮
6	新	
7	好	
8	張	弓（ㄱ ㄱ 弓 ）
		長（一 丆 丆 丐 丐 丟 丟 長 ）
9	紙	
10	小	
11	大	一 ナ 大
12	多	夕
		夕

13	少	小 少
14	北	丨 丬 ⺦ 北 北
15	京	丶 亠 古 京
16	旧	丨 旧

Lesson 15

生詞 Shēngcí New Words
SIDE FOUR, BAND SIX

1.	的	(助) dē	(a structural particle)
2.	同志	(名) tóngzhì	comrade
3.	俄文	(名) èwén	the Russian language
4.	朋友	(名) péngyǒu	friend
5.	干淨	(形) gānjìng	clean
6.	我們	(代) wǒmén	we, us
7.	你們	(代) nǐmén	you
8.	他們	(代) tāmén	they, them
9.	她	(代) tā	she, her
10.	它	(代) tā	it
11.	枝	(量) zhī	(a measure word)
12.	鉛笔	(名) qiānbǐ [枝]	pencil
13.	長	(形) cháng	long
14.	短	(形) duǎn	short
15.	黑板	(名) hēibǎn	blackboard

語法 Yǔfǎ Grammar

15.1 The Structural Particle 的 (1) We know already that adjectives may modify nouns, an adjective modifier is an adjective modifying a noun (14.4), and the noun modified is called the central word. Besides adjectives, nouns, pronouns and words of other parts of speech and even constructions (phrases) may all be used as adjective modifiers. Here in this lesson we will consider nouns, pronouns and adjectives used as adjective modifiers. An adjective modifier must precede the central word or the word it modifies, and the structural particle 的 is often used in between. e. g.

1. 先生的　书　很　多.
   Xiānshēngde　shū　hěn　duō.

   The teacher has very many books. (LIT.: The teacher's books are very many.)

2. 这　是　他的　纸.
   Zhèi　shì　tāde　zhǐ.

   This is his paper.

3. 他　是　一个　很　好的　同志.
   Tā　shì　yíge　hěn　hǎode　tóngzhì.

   He is a very good comrade.

书, 纸, and 同志 are central words, 先生, 他 and 好 are adjective modifiers; there exists between the adjective modifier and the central word a relation of ownership (as in examples 1, 2) or a descriptive relationship (as in example 3). An adjective modifier of ownership can only be formed by a noun or a pronoun, while an adjective modifier made up of an adjective is always used to modify or describe the central word.

It is not quite true that after an adjective modifier there must be a structural particle 的. From the following rules we see when it has to be used or when not.

(1) Some nouns and pronouns used as adjective modifiers are so integral a part of their central words that they have become stable word groups. In such cases, we do not use the particle 的. e. g.

4. 中国　人
   Zhōngguó　rén

   (a) Chinese (person)

5. 俄文　报
   èwén   bào

(a) Russian newspaper

6. 我　　朋友
  wǒ   péngyǒu

my friend

(2) When adjectives, especially monosyllabic ones, are used as adjective modifiers, we do not use the particle 的 in general. e. g.

7. 好　学生
  hǎo xuéshêng

(a) good student

8. 旧　書
  jiù shū

(an) old book

9. 干淨　紙
  gānjìng zhǐ

clean paper

But, when the adjective is modified by an adverbial modifier, the particle 的 is generally indispensable (the adjectives 多 and 少 are exceptions). e. g.

10. 很　旧的　报
  hěn jiùdě bào

(a) very old newspaper

11. 不　好的　書
  bù hǎodě shū

(a) book that is not good

12. 很　干淨的　紙
  hěn gānjìngdě zhǐ

very clean paper

(3) When it is clear from the context what the central word should be, the central word may be omitted, but the particle 的 must on no account be left out after the adjective modifier. e. g.

13. 这本 新 书 干净, 那本 旧的 不 干净.
　　Zhèiběn xīn shū gānjìng, nèiběn jiùdé bù gānjìng.

This new book is clean, that old one is not clean.

We say 旧的 instead of 旧书, because the idea of 书 is already expressed by 新书.

15.2 The Arrangement of Adjective Modifiers　　Numerals in conjunction with measure words used before nouns (such as 一本书) and demonstrative pronouns in conjunction with measure words or with numerals and measure words used before nouns (such as 这本书 and 这三本书) are also adjective modifiers (with the exception of nouns used as measure words, all measure words are used without 的). When an adjective modifier is composed of a demonstrative pronoun, a numeral and a measure word, the demonstrative pronoun stands first, then the numeral and the measure word (14.1).　When the modifier contains not only the three elements mentioned above, but also a personal pronoun, a noun or an adjective, the word order is as follows:

(1) In an adj. modifier, the adjective should be near the central word. e. g.

14. 那　　一本　新　书
　　nèi　yìběn　xīn　shū

that new book

15. 这　　一張　旧　报
　　zhèi　yìzhāng　jiù　bào

this old newspaper

(2) The personal pronoun must always stand before the demonstrative pronoun, therefore an adjective modifier of ownership composed of a personal pronoun or a noun must always come first. e. g.

16. <u>他的</u> 那 一張 旧 报
    tādě nèi yìzhāng jiù bào

that old newspaper of his (LIT.: his that one sheet old newspaper)

17. <u>先生的</u> 这 一本 新 書
    xiānshěngdě zhèi yìběn xīn shū

this new book of the teacher's

15.3 The Interrogative Sentence (2)   The second kind of the interrogative sentence is alternative in form, including both the affirmative and the negative sides of a thing set side by side; in other words, the alternative form includes both the affirmative and the negative forms of the predicate. The person trying to answer the question is expected to choose between the two. In the sentence with a substantive predicate (1), the alternative form is 是不是. e. g.

18. 他 <u>是 不 是</u> 先生?
    Tā shì bú shì xiānshěng?

Is he a teacher? (LIT.: He is, not is, a teacher?)

19. 这 <u>是 不 是</u> 报?
    Zhèi shì bú shì bào?

Is this a newspaper (or isn't it)?

不是 may also stand at the end of a sentence .e. g.

20. 他 是 先生 <u>不 是</u>?
    Tā shì xiānshěng bú shì?

Is he a teacher? (LIT.: He is a teacher, not is?)

21. 这 是 报 <u>不 是</u>?
    Zhèi shì bào bú shì?

Is this a newspaper?

In the sentence with an adjectival predicate, the alternative form includes both the affirmative and the negative forms of the predicative adjective. e. g.

22. 这本　书　好　不　好?
Zhèiběn　shū　hǎo　bù　hǎo?
Is this book good (or not)?

23. 那張　紙　干淨　不　干淨?
Nèizhāng　zhǐ　gānjǐng　bù　gānjǐng?
Is that paper clean (or not)?

15.4 們　們 is a suffix indicating plural number. All singular personal pronouns with 們 are plural in number. e. g.

24. 我——我們
wǒ——wǒmén
I ----- we (OR: me ----- us)

25. 你——你們
nǐ —— nǐmén

you (singular) --- you (plural)

(們 is, in general, not used after 您 to indicate plural number.)

26. 他——他們
tā —— tāmén
he ---- they (OR: him ---- them)

"們" may also be used after nouns indicating plural number, but attention should be paid to the following two points:

(1) 們 is only used after nouns denoting persons, such as 先生們, 学生們 etc. The other nouns cannot take such a suffix. We cannot say 書們, 报們 etc.

(2) A noun followed by the suffix 們 is always plural, but a noun without such a suffix may be either singular or plural. When it is clearly shown by context that the noun is in the plural, it is no longer necessary to use the suffix. e. g.

27. 我們　是　学生.
Wǒmén　shì　xuéshēng.
We are students.

28. 很 多 先生 是 北京 人.
Hěn duō xiānshēng shì Běijīng rén.

(Very) many teachers are from Peking.

Because 我們 and 很多 already imply that 學生, 先生 and 北京
人 are in the plural, we no longer use the suffix 們. According
to the above, 們 is used only when there is absolute necessity
and when there is no other indication of plurality.

15.5 她 and 它 These two words have the same pronunciation as 他, and are also pronouns of the third person singular. In writing, 他 may be used to indicate any person or
thing of the third person singular. But now we always use 他
to denote the male, 她 the female and 它 all things or matters
exclusive of human beings. 她 is the same as 他 in use, but
它 should never be used at the beginning of a sentence. We can
say 她是先生, but we must never say 它是紙. Moreover, the
word 它 cannot, in general, be followed by 們 to indicate plural
number.

課文 Kèwén Text

SIDE FOUR, BAND SIX

I

1. 我 朋友的 書 很 多.
Wǒ péngyǒudě shū hěn duō.

My friend has many books. (LIT.: My friend's books
are very many.)

2. 她的 書 很 新.
Tādě shū hěn xīn.

Her books are (very) new.

II

3. 这 是 一枝 新 鉛筆.
Zhèi shì yìzhī xīn qiānbǐ.

This is a new pencil.

4. 这枝　鉛笔　很　長.
Zhèizhī qiānbǐ hěn cháng.
This pencil is (very) long.

5. 新　鉛笔　長, 旧　鉛笔　短.
Xīn qiānbǐ cháng, jiù qiānbǐ duǎn.
The new pencil is long, the old pencil is short.

III

(a₁) 这　是　黑板　不　是?
Zhèi shì hēibǎn bú shì?
Is this a blackboard (or is it not)?

(b₁) 这　是　黑板.
Zhèi shì hēibǎn.
This is a blackboard. (= Yes.)

(a₂) 这个　黑板　干淨　不　干淨?
Zhèigě hēibǎn gānjǐng bù gānjǐng?
Is this blackboard clean (or not clean)?

(b₂) 很　干淨, 这　是　一个　新
Hěn gānjǐng, zhèi shì yígě xīn
黑板. 新的　干淨, 旧的　不
hēibǎn. Xīndě gānjǐng, jiùdě bù
干淨.
gānjǐng.

(It is) very clean; this is a new blackboard. The new one is clean, the old one is not.

(a₃) 你們的　先生　是　中国　人　嗎?
Nǐměndě xiānshēng shì Zhōngguó rén mǎ?

Is your teacher Chinese?

(b₃) 是　中国　人.
Shì Zhōngguó rén.
Yes. (LIT.: Is Chinese.)

(a₄) 你們的　　先生　多　不　多?
　　　Nǐmĕndĕ　xiānshĕng　duō　bù　duō?

Do you have many teachers? (LIT.: Your teachers many not many?)

(b₄) 很　多.
　　　Hĕn　duō.

Yes.

(a₅) 那个　　同志　　是　不　是　你們的
　　　Nèigĕ　tóngzhì　shì　bú　shì　nǐmĕndĕ
先生?
xiānshĕng?

Is that comrade your teacher?

(b₅) 是, 她　是　我們的　　先生. 她　很
　　　Shì, tā　shì　wŏmĕndĕ　xiānshĕng. Tā　hĕn
好, 她　是　一个　　很　好的　先生.
hǎo, tā　shì　yígĕ　hĕn　hǎodĕ　xiānshĕng.

Yes, she is our teacher. She is very good; she is a very good teacher.

課外練習　Kèwài liànxí　Home Work

1) Copy all the new words once.

2) The following words and word groups can all be used as adjective modifiers of nouns, so please fill the blanks with proper nouns (pay attention to the use and omission of the particle 的):

(1) 她們＿＿＿　(2) 朋友＿＿＿　(3) 旧　＿＿＿

(4) 干淨＿＿＿　(5) 很 長＿＿＿　(6) 不 好＿＿＿

3) Change the following questions into alternative interrogative sentences, and write answers to all of them:

(7) 这个　黑板　大　嗎?

(8) 那　是　先生的　紙　嗎?

(9) 他　那枝　鉛笔　長　嗎?

(10) 您的　那个　朋友　是　一个　新　学生
嗎?

五、汉字表　Hànzì biǎo　Chinese Characters

1	的	
2	同	
3	志	
4	俄	亻
		我
5	文	
6	朋	月 ( ) 刀 月 月)
		月
7	友	一 ナ 友
8	干	一 干
9	淨	氵
		爭 (ノ ⼂ ⺈ ⺈ 爫 爭 爭 爭)
10	們	
11	她	女
		也

12	它	宀
		匕
13	枝	木
		支（十支）
14	鉛	
15	笔	
16	長	
17	短	矢
		豆（一口口豆豆）
18	黑	丨 冂 冂 冂 四 罒 里 里 黑
19	板	木
		反

Lesson 16

生詞　Shēngcí　New Words
SIDE FOUR, BAND SEVEN

1. 工作　　(动、名) gōngzuò　to work, work

2. 学習　　(动) xuéxí　　to study

3. 教　　　(动) jiāo　　to teach

4. 中文　　(名) zhōngwén　the Chinese language

5. 給　　　(动) gěi　　to give

6. 看　　　(动) kàn　　to see, to look at

7. 来　　　(动) lái　　to come

8. 有　　　(动) yǒu　　to have

9. 没　　　(副) méi　　not

10. 只　　　(副) zhǐ　　only

11. 本子　　(名) běnzi [本] note-book

語法　Yǔfǎ　Grammar

16.1 The Sentence with a Verbal Predicate　　A sentence in which the predicate is composed of a verb is called the sentence with a verbal predicate. A verb is a word that describes some action, behaviour or change. In the sentence with a verbal predicate, the predicate tells about the action, behaviour or change of the person or thing denoted by the subject. The sentence with a verbal predicate may be divided into three kinds:

(1) The simple verbal sentence   This is the kind of sentence where there is only a verb and no object, that is to say, the predicate of such a sentence is formed by the verb itself. e. g.

1. 先生　工作.
Xiānshēng gōngzuò.
The teacher works.

2. 我們　学習.
Wǒmen　xuéxí.
We study.

(2) The verbal sentence with a single object   This is the kind of sentence where the predicate is made up of a verb and its object. The verb precedes the object. e. g.

3. 先生　教　我.
Xiānshēng jiāo　wǒ.
The teacher teaches me.

4. 我們　学習　中文.
Wǒmen　xuéxí　zhōngwén.
We study Chinese.

先生 and 我們 are subjects, 教 and 学習 are verbs, and 我 and 中文 are objects. The subject precedes the predicate. The following word order is recognized as the basic construction of the verbal sentence:

Subject — Verb — Object

(3) The verbal sentence with double object   This is the kind of sentence where there may be one verb and two objects in the predicate. Such a sentence is called the verbal sentence with double object. The verb precedes the objects, and the indirect object (which in general denotes some person) precedes the direct object (which in general denotes some thing).e. g.

5. 先生　教　我　中文.
Xiānshēng jiāo　wǒ　zhōngwén.
The teacher teaches me Chinese.

6. 他　　給　　朋友　　一枝　　鉛笔.
   Tā　gěi　péngyǒu　yìzhī　qiānbǐ.
   He gives his friend a (one) pencil.

先生 and 他 are subjects, 教 and 給 are verbs. 中文 and 鉛笔 are direct objects, while 我 and 朋友 are indirect objects. Therefore, the word order of the verbal sentence with double object is as follows:

Subject — Verb — Indirect Object — Direct Object

In example 6, the object (or the noun 鉛笔) is preceded by an adjective modifier made up of a numeral and a measure word 一枝. In fact, all the subjects and objects in such sentences can be preceded by adjective modifiers. In the following example, the subject and the objects all have adjective modifiers:

7. 我們　　先生　　給　　那个　　学生　　一本
   Wǒmén　xiānshéng　gěi　nèigė　xuéshéng　yìběn
   很　　新的　　書.
   hěn　xīndė　shū.
   Our teacher gives that student a very new book.

16.2 The Negative Form of the Sentence with a Verbal Predicate   Just like the negative forms of the sentence with a substantive predicate and the sentence with an adjectival predicate, we use the negative adverb 不 to form the negative of the sentence with a verbal predicate. When we put the adverb 不 before the verb, it means "used not to do so", "shall or will not do so" or "to be not willing to do so". e. g.

8. 我　　不　　看　　这張　　旧　　报.
   Wǒ　bú　kàn　zhèizhāng　jiù　bào.
   I do not read this old newspaper.

9. 我的　　朋友　　不　　来.
   Wǒdė　péngyǒu　bù　lái.
   My friend is not coming (or: does not come).

10. 她　　不　　給　　我　　那張　　纸.
    Tā　bù　gěi　wǒ　nèizhāng　zhǐ.
    She is not giving me (or: does not give me) that sheet of paper.

16.3 The Negative Form of 有 The word 有 is a rather special verb, its negative form is 沒有 and not 不有. e. g.

11. 我　沒　有　鉛笔.
Wǒ　méi　yǒu　qiānbǐ.
I do not have a pencil.

12. 先生　沒　有　俄文　报.
Xiānshēng　méi　yǒu　èwén　bào.
The teacher does not have a Russian newspaper.

When there is some other element following 沒有, 沒有 can be simplified as 沒 only. But at the end of a sentence, we must say 沒有. e. g.

13. 你們　有　書　嗎?
Nǐmén　yǒu　shū　mǎ?
Do you (plural) have books?

14. 他　有　書,　我　沒　書.
Tā　yǒu　shū,　wǒ　méi　shū.
（or:　我　沒　有.）
　　　　Wǒ　méi　yǒu.
He has a book, I do not have a book (OR: I don't have).

16.4 How to Change a Sentence with a Verbal Predicate into an Interrogative Sentence Such a sentence is changed into an interrogative sentence either by adding the particle 嗎, or by using the alternative form e. g.

15. 你　来　嗎?
Nǐ　lái　mǎ?
Are you coming?

16. 你　不　来　嗎?
Nǐ　bù　lái　mǎ?
Aren't you coming?

17. 你　来　不　来?
Nǐ　lái　bù　lái?
Are you coming (or not)?

When there is an object, this is the word order of the alternative interrogative sentence: the object may stand after the verbs or between the affirmative verb and the negative verb (refer to the alternative interrogative form of the sentence with a substantive predicate (1)). e. g.

18. 你們　學習　不　学習　俄文?
Nǐmén　xuéxí　bù　xuéxí　èwén?
Do you (plural) study Russian?

19. 你們　学習　俄文　不　学習?
Nǐmén　xuéxí　èwén　bù　xuéxí?
Do you (plural) study Russian?

20. 那个　同志　教　不　教　你們　中文?
Nèigè　tóngzhì　jiāo　bù　jiāo　nǐmén　zhōngwén?
Does that comrade teach you (plural) Chinese?

21. 那个　同志　教　你們　中文　不　教?
Nèigè　tóngzhì　jiāo　nǐmén　zhōngwén　bù　jiāo?
Does that comrade teach you (plural) Chinese (or not)?

If the verb is 有, we have to use the form 有沒有 ... or the form 有 ...沒有. e. g.

22. 他　有　沒　有　鉛笔?
Tā　yǒu　méi　yǒu　qiānbǐ?
Does he have a pencil?

23. 他　有　鉛笔　沒　有?
Tā　yǒu　qiānbǐ　méi　yǒu?
Does he have a pencil?

課文　Kèwén　Text
SIDE FOUR, BAND SEVEN

I

(a₁) 您　来　不　来?
Nín　lái　bù　lái?
Are you (formal) coming?

(b₁) 我 来, 您 来 吗?
Wǒ lái, nín lái mǎ?

Yes, are you (formal)?

(a₂) 我 不 来.
Wǒ bù lái.

No.

II

(a₃) 他 看 俄文 書 吗?
Tā kàn èwén shū mǎ?

Does he read Russian books?

(b₃) 他 不 看, 他 只 看 中文 書.
Tā bú kàn, tā zhǐ kàn zhōngwén shū.

No, he reads only Chinese books.

(a₄) 您 看 俄文 書 不 看?
Nín kàn èwén shū bú kàn?

Do you (formal) read Russian books?

(b₄) 我 看, 我 学習 俄文, 我 有 很
Wǒ kàn, wǒ xuéxí èwén, wǒ yǒu hěn

多 俄文 書.
duō èwén shū.

Yes; I am studying Russian and I have many Russian
books.

III

(a₅) 这个 先生 教 不 教 你?
Zhèigê xiānshêng jiāo bù jiāo nǐ?

Is this teacher your instructor? (LIT.: This teacher
teaches not teaches you?)

(b₅) 教 我, 她 教 我們 中文.
Jiāo wǒ, tā jiāo wǒmên zhōngwén.

Yes, she is our Chinese instructor. (LIT.: Teaches me,
she teaches us Chinese.)

(a₆) 她　教　俄文　不　教?
Tā　jiāo　èwén　bù　jiāo?
Does she teach Russian?

(b₆) 她　不　教　俄文，只　教　中文.
Tā　bù　jiāo　èwén，　zhǐ　jiāo　zhōngwén.
She doesn't teach Russian, she teaches only Chinese.

(a₇) 她　教　他們　不　教?
Tā　jiāo　tāmén　bù　jiāo?
Is she their instructor? (LIT.: Does she teach them not teach?)

(b₇) 不　教，她　只　教　新　学生.
Bù　jiāo，　tā　zhǐ　jiāo　xīn　xuéshēng.
No, she teaches only new students.

(a₈) 您的　朋友　有　本子　嗎?
Níndê　péngyǒu　yǒu　běnzǐ　mǎ?
Does your friend have a notebook?

(b₈) 有　本子，他的　本子　很　多.
Yǒu　běnzǐ，　tādê　běnzǐ　hěn　duō.
Yes, he has many notebooks.

(a₉) 那个　学生　有　本子　沒　有?
Nèigê　xuéshēng　yǒu　běnzǐ　méi　yǒu?
Does that student have a notebook?

(b₉) 沒　有，他　有　紙.
Méi　yǒu，　tā　yǒu　zhǐ.
No, he has paper.

課外練習　Kèwài liànxí　Home Work

1) Copy all the new words in this lesson once.

2) Make sentences with each of the following verbs:

(1) 工作　　　(2) 有　　　(3) 給

3) Copy the following sentences and underline the subjects,

the adjective modifiers, the verbs, and the direct objects and indirect objects:

For example:

那个　先生　教　我　中文.

(4) 这个　先生　来, 那个　先生　不　来.

(5) 您的　朋友　看　中文　报, 我的　朋友　看　俄文　报.

(6) 先生　給　学生　一本　新　書.

4) Answer the questions in the negative:

(7) 你　有　干淨的　紙　嗎?

(8) 那个　学生　看　俄文　書　不　看?

汉字表　Hànzì biǎo　Chinese Characters

1	工	一 丁 工
2	作	
3	習	羽 (丁 习 习 羽)
		白
4	教	考 (土 耂 考)
		攵
5	給	糹
		合
6	看	手 (丿 二 三 手)
		目 (丨 冂 冃 月 目)

7	来	一 ㇠ ㇗ 丑 丰 耒 来
8	有	一 ナ 有
9	沒	冫 氵 汐 沒
10	只	
11	子	

Lesson 17

生詞 Shēngcí New Words
SIDE FIVE, BAND ONE

1. 鋼笔 (名) gāngbǐ pen
2. 都 (副) dōu all
3. 也 (副) yě also, too
4. 桌子 (名) zhuōzǐ [張] table
5. 和 (連) hé and
6. 把 (量) bǎ (a measure word)
7. 椅子 (名) yǐzǐ [把] chair
8. 杂誌 (名) zázhì [本] magazine
9. 画报 (名) huàbào [本] pictorial
10. 北京大学 (名) Běijīngdàxué Peking University
11. 会 (动) huì to know how to do
12. 对了 duìlê yes, that is right
13. 有意思 yǒuyìsi interesting

語法 Yǔfǎ Grammar

17.1 The Sentence with a Substantive Predicate (2)   Nouns, pronouns and adjectives may all be used as adjective modifiers to modify nouns (15.1), therefore in the sentence with a substantive predicate (1), when the predicate is made up of a noun, it may carry any of these adjective modifiers. e. g.

1. 这本　書　是　先生的　書.
Zhèiběn　shū　shì　xiānshéngdė　shū.
This book is the teacher's book.

2. 那枝　鋼笔　是　我的　鋼笔.
Nèizhī　gāngbǐ　shì　wǒdė　gāngbǐ.
That (fountain) pen is my (fountain) pen.

3. 这个　本子　是　新　本子.
Zhèigė　běnzǐ　shì　xīn　běnzi.
This notebook is a new notebook.

We have already learned that the central word (or the word modified) may be omitted, if the context is clear without it (15.1), so all the above sentences may be recast as follows:

4. 这本　書　是　先生的.
Zhèiběn　shū　shì　xiānshéngdė.
This book is the teacher's.

5. 那枝　鋼笔　是　我的.
Nèizhī　gāngbǐ　shì　wǒdė.
That pen is mine.

6. 这个　本子　是　新的.
Zhèigė　běnzǐ　shì　xīndė.
This notebook is a new one.

Here, all the substantives used as central words (all of them being nouns: 書, 鋼笔, and 本子) have been omitted, but the noun, pronoun or adjective in the adjective modifiers may, together with the structural particle 的, assume the function of a substantive (先生的, 我的 or 新的). This is called the substantive construction. A sentence, in which the main element of the predicate is composed of such a substantive construction, is called the sentence with a substantive predicate (2).

With the exception of the chief element of the predicate which is composed of a substantive construction, the sentence with a substantive predicate (2) is essentially the same as the sentence with a substantive predicate (1). So far as the sentence structure is concerned, in the sentence of the second kind, the copula 是 is also required to connect the subject with the chief element of the predicate. As for its function, the predicate of the second kind is to explain the person or thing denoted by the subject. But speaking more in detail, the predicate of the second kind describes the quality of the person or thing denoted by the subject, or the kind of person or thing.

17.2 The Negative Form of the Sentence with a Substantive Predicate (2) We put the negative adverb 不 before the copula 是 to negate the sentence with a substantive predicate (1) as has been explained before. Here we do the same to negate the sentence with a substantive predicate (2). e. g.

7. 这本　書　是　先生的　嗎？
Zhèiběn　shū　shì　xiānshêngdê　mǎ?
Is this book the teacher's?

8. 这本　書　不　是　先生的.
Zhèiběn　shū　bú　shì　xiānshêngdê.
This book is not the teacher's.

9. 那張　紙　是　不　是　你的？
Nèizhāng　zhǐ　shì　bú　shì　nídê?
Is that sheet of paper yours (or not)?

10. 不　是, 那張　紙　不　是　我的.
Bú　shì, nèizhāng　zhǐ　bú　shì　wǒdê.
No, that sheet of paper is not mine.

11. 那个　本子　是　不　是　新的？
Nèigê　běnzî　shì　bú　shì　xīndê?
Is that notebook a new one?

12. 不　是　新的.
Bú　shì　xīndê.
No (it is not a new one).

Note: The method of asking questions is the same as explained under the sentence with a substantive predicate (1).

17.3 都 and 也   We know that 不 is an adverb of negation, 很 is an adverb of degree and 只 is an adverb of extent. Now, 都 is also an adverb of extent. As far as the meaning is concerned, it refers to the persons and things that have already appeared in the same sentence; its place in the syntax is after the subject and before the predicate. e. g.

13. 先生　都　是　中国　人.
　　Xiānshěng dōu shì Zhōngguó rén.
　　All the teachers are Chinese.

14. 她的　書　都　是　俄文的.
　　Tādě shū dōu shì èwéndě.
　　All her books are Russian ones.

Note: In Chinese, when a plural noun is used as subject, the plural number is always expressed by the adverb 都. Although example 13 may be changed into 先生們都是中国人, yet it would be not idiomatic if we say 先生們是中国人. In example 14, the plural number of 書 is of course expressed by the adverb 都.

"也" is also an adverb, and like the adverb "都" it has to be put before the predicate. e. g.

15. 这本　書　好, 那本　書　也　好.
　　Zhèiběn shū hǎo, nèiběn shū yě hǎo.
　　This book is good, that book is also good.

16. 我　看　报, 他　也　看　报.
　　Wǒ kàn bào, tā yě kàn bào.
　　I read newspapers, he also reads newspapers.

We must not say 也那本書 or 也他. Similarly, it is not correct to say 都先生 and 都她的書.

In general, adverbs, especially when monosyllabic, are not used as predicates, therefore they cannot be used to answer questions by themselves (the negative adverb 不 is an exception), for they must be affixed to verbs or adjectives. 都 and 也 come under the same rule. e. g.

17. 你的　朋友　都　来　吗?
Nǐdě　péngyǒu　dōu　lái　mǎ?

Are all your friends coming?

18. 都　来.
Dōu　lái.

Yes (they are all coming).

19. 黑板　很　干淨,　桌子　也　很　干淨　吗?
Hēibǎn　hěn　gānjǐng,　zhuōzǐ　yě　hěn　gānjǐng　mǎ?

The blackboard is very clean; is the table very clean too?

20. 也　很　干淨.
Yě　hěn　gānjǐng.

Yes (it is very clean too).

When 都 and 也 are used together, the general rule is that 也 precedes 都. e. g.

21. 我們　是　学生,　他們　也　都　是　学生.
Wǒmen　shì　xuéshěng,　tāmen　yě　dōu　shì　xuéshěng.

We are students, they are all students too.

17.4 和　The chief function of this conjunction is to connect nouns and pronouns. e. g.

22. 这本　書　和　那本　書　都　好.
Zhèiběn　shū　hé　nèiběn　shū　dōu　hǎo.

This book and that book are both good.

23. 她　和　那个　同志　都　是　我的　朋友.
Tā　hé　nèigě　tóngzhì　dōu　shì　wǒdě　péngyǒu.

She and that comrade are both my friends.

24. 我　和　他　都　不　是　先生.
Wǒ　hé　tā　dōu　bú　shì　xiānshěng.

He and I are both not teachers. (LIT.: I and he all not are teachers.)

But in Chinese, not all nouns and pronouns are connected by conjunctions, particularly when two nouns stand together. There, we often use a pause instead of a conjunction. e. g.

25. 这本　書、那本　書　都　好.
Zhèiběn　shū、　nèiběn　shū　dōu　hǎo.

This book (and) that book are both good.

26. 先生、学生　都　来.
Xiānshěng、xuéshěng　dōu　lái.

The teachers (and) students are all coming.

課文　Kèwén　Text

SIDE FIVE, BAND ONE

I

(a₁)　这張　桌子　是　您的　嗎?
Zhèizhāng　zhuōzi　shì　níndě　mǎ?

Is this table yours (formal)?

(b₁)　不　是，这張　桌子　是　我　朋友-
Bú　shì，zhèizhāng　zhuōzi　shì　wǒ　péngyǒu-
的.
dě.

No, this table is my friend's.

(a₂)　这把　椅子　是　您的　不　是?
Zhèibǎ　yǐzi　shì　níndě　bú　shì?

Is this chair yours (formal)?

(b₂)　也　不　是，这把　椅子　也　是
Yě　bú　shì，zhèibǎ　yǐzi　yě　shì
她的.
tādě.

It's not mine, either; this chair is hers too.

(a₃) 她   这本   杂誌   和   这本   画报   都
　　　Tā   zhèiběn zázhì   hé   zhèiběn huàbào dōu

　　　是   新的   吗?
　　　shì   xīndě   mǎ?

Are this magazine of hers and this picture news magazine (both) new?

(b₃) 都   是   新的,   她的   杂誌、   画报   都
　　　Dōu   shì   xīndě,   tādě   zázhì、   huàbào dōu

　　　是   新的.
　　　shì   xīndě.

Yes, her magazine and picture news magazine are (both) new.

(a₄) 那个   先生   和   那个   学生   都   是
　　　Nèige xiānshēng hé   nèige xuéshēng dōu shì

　　　北京   大学的   吗?
　　　Běijīng Dàxuédě mǎ?

Do that teacher and that student (both) belong to Peking University?

(b₄) 都   是   北京   大学的.
　　　Dōu   shì   Běijīng Dàxuédě.

Yes. (They both belong to Peking University.)

(a₅) 你們   也   都   是   北京   大学的   吗?
　　　Nǐmen yě   dōu   shì   Běijīng Dàxuédě mǎ?

Do you also belong to Peking University?

(b₅) 不   都   是,   我是,   他   不   是.
　　　Bù   dōu   shì,   wǒ shì, tā   bú   shì.

Not both of us; I do, but he doesn't.

II

(a₆) 这本　　杂誌　是　中文的　　吗?
Zhèibĕn zázhì shì zhōngwéndê må?

Is this magazine Chinese?

(b₆) 不　是　中文的,　是　俄文的.
Bú shì zhōngwéndê, shì èwéndê.

我　不　会　中文.
Wŏ bú huì zhōngwén.

No, it's Russian. I don't know Chinese.

(a₇) 那本　画报　也　是　俄文的　　吗?
Nèibĕn huàbào yĕ shì èwéndê må?

Is that picture news magazine Russian too?

(b₇) 不　是　俄文的,　是　中文的.
Bú shì èwéndê, shì zhōngwéndê.

No, it's Chinese.

(a₈) 你　看　中文　画报　吗?
Nǐ kàn zhōngwén huàbào må?

Do you read Chinese picture news magazines?

(b₈) 对　了,　我　看　中文　画报.
Duì lê, wŏ kàn zhōngwén huàbào.

That's right, I do.

(a₉) 你的　朋友　也　都　看　中文　画报
Nǐdê péngyŏu yĕ, dōu kàn zhōngwén huàbào

吗?
må?

Do your friends (all) read Chinese picture news magazines too?

(b₉) 他們　也　都　看　中文　画报.
Tāmen　yě　dōu　kàn　zhōngwén　huàbào.

中文　画报　很　有意思.
Zhōngwén　huàbào　hěn　yǒuyìsì.

Yes, they do too. Chinese picture news magazines are
very interesting.

(a₁₀) 你們　只　看　中文　画报　嗎?
Nímen　zhǐ　kàn　zhōngwén　huàbào　må?

Do you read Chinese picture news magazines only?

(b₁₀) 不,　我們　也　看　俄文　画报.
Bù,　wǒmen　yě　kàn　èwén　huàbào.

No, we read Russian picture news magazines too.

課外練習　Kèwài liànxí　Home Work

1) Translate and answer the following questions:—
(1) Are all your books and magazines new?
(2) Do these three students belong to Peking University?
(3) Are this magazine and that pictorial yours?
(4) Does that new pencil belong to your friend or not?

2) Change the following phonetic spellings into Chinese
characters and write down the answers:
(5) Xiānshěngdě huàbào yǒuyìsì méi yǒu?
(6) Zhèibǎ yǐzì shì bú shì jiùdě?
(7) Nǐměndě xiānshěng huì bú huì èwén?

汉字表　Hànzì biǎo　Chinese Characters

1	鋼	金	
		岡（冂冂冂冂冈冈冈冈）	
2	都	者（土耂者）	
		阝	
3	也		
4	桌	丨卜占桌	
5	和	禾（丿禾）	
		口	
6	把	扌	
		巴（フ刀コ巴）	
7	椅	木	
		奇	大
			可（一口可）
8	杂	九（丿九）	
		朩	
9	誌	言	
		志	
10	画		
11	会	人	

		云 （ ` 二 云 ）
12	对	
13	了	⁻ 了
14	意	立
		曰
		心
15	思	田
		心

Lesson 18

語法复習   Yǔfǎ fùxí   Review

18.1 The Sentence with a Substantive Predicate (1) and the Sentence with a Substantive Predicate (2)   We have already learned the sentence with a substantive predicate (1) (13.1). The syntax of the sentence is as follows:

Subject——Copula——Substantive.

For example:

1. 他　是　先生.
   Tā　shì　xiānshēng.

   He is a teacher.

2. 这　是　报.
   Zhèi　shì　bào.

   This is a newspaper.

Examples 1 and 2 are all simple sentences with substantive predicate (1), for after each 是, there is only a simple substantive. We know that nouns may take adjective modifiers, such sentences are rather complicated. e. g.

3. 那个　中国　学生　是　新　学生.
   Nèige　Zhōngguó　xuéshēng　shì　xīn　xuéshēng.

   That Chinese student is a new student.

4. 很 多　中国　学生　是　我們的　好
　Hěn duō Zhōngguó xuéshêng shì wǒmêndê hǎo

朋友.
péngyǒu.

(Very) many Chinese students are good friends of ours.

Since substantives include nouns, pronouns, numerals and measure words, it is beyond question that pronouns, numerals and measure words may be used after 是. When a demonstrative pronoun, a numeral and a measure word make up the chief element of the predicate of a sentence, the whole sentence will also appear more or less complicated. e. g.

5. 我的　書　是　这　一本,　你的　是
　Wǒdê shū shì zhèi yìběn, nǐdê shì

那　一本.
nèi yìběn.

My book is this one, yours is that one.

In examples 3,4 and 5, the elements after 是 are word groups: the first two are made up of nouns and their adjective modifiers, and the last one is a combination of a pronoun, a numeral and a measure word. Such sentences are still sentences with substantive predicates (1). Therefore whether the substantive after 是 is a single word or a word group does not make it a different kind of sentence. So long as the sentence is in agreement with the word order given above, it is called the sentence with a substantive predicate (1). So far as the function of such kind of sentence is concerned, the predicate is used to describe the person or thing denoted by the subject.

We have also learned the sentence with a substantive predicate (2) (17.1). The word order of this kind of sentence is as follows:

Subject — Copula — Substantive Construction (a noun, pronoun or adjective + "的")

In the sentence with a substantive predicate (2), the noun, pronoun or adjective and 的 after the copula form a substantive construction or its equivalent describing the quality of the person or thing denoted by the subject, or the kind of the person or thing. e. g.

6. 他的　　杂誌　　是　　中文的.
   Tādě　　zázhì　　shì　　zhōngwéndě.

   His magazine is a Chinese one.

7. 那本　　新　　書　　是　　他的.
   Nèiběn　　xīn　　shū　　shì　　tādě.

   That new book is his.

8. 这張　　紙　　是　　干淨的.
   Zhèizhāng　　zhǐ　　shì　　gānjìngdě.

   This sheet of paper is a clean one.

Two points have to be noticed, when we use the sentence with a substantive predicate:

(1) In the predicate, the copula has to be used. We cannot say 我学生 or 这張桌子干淨的.

(2) In the sentence with a substantive predicate (2), we should use …是…的 and the word 的 should never be omitted. We must say 这本杂誌是旧的, and we never say 这本杂誌是旧.

18.2 **The Sentence with an Adjectival Predicate and the Sentence with a Substantive Predicate (2)**　　We have already learned the sentence with an adjectival predicate (14.3), let us look at the following examples:

9. 这个　　黑板　　很　　大.
   Zhèigě　　hēibǎn　　hěn　　dà.

   This blackboard is very big.

10. 这个　　黑板　　很　　干淨.
    Zhèigě　　hēibǎn　　hěn　　gānjìng.

    This blackboard is very clean.

The predicates of the above examples, 大 and 干淨, are made up of adjectives. Such sentences are called sentences with adjectival predicates, because the predicates are made up of adjectives. Now let us look at more examples:

11. 这个　黑板　是　大的.
Zhèigè　hēibǎn　shì　dàdê.
This blackboard is a big one.

12. 这个　黑板　是　干淨的.
Zhèigè　hēibǎn　shì　gānjìngdê.
This blackboard is a clean one.

Although the words 大 and 干淨 are adjectives, with the use of 的, they have become substantive constructions. Therefore, the two sentences given above are sentences with substantive predicates (2).

There are marked differences between the sentence with an adjectival predicate and the sentence with a substantive predicate (2):

(1) The copula 是 can never be used before the predicate in the sentence with an adjectival predicate (14.3), should always be used in the predicate of the sentence with a substantive predicate (13.1, 17.1, 18.1).

(2) The adjective in the sentence with an adjectival predicate is descriptive in function; while in the sentence with a substantive predicate, the adjective with 的 is a substantive construction, which in conjunction with the copula, becomes a complete predicate, assuming the function of judgement or explanation.

According to the above, the sentence with an adjectival predicate is used for the purpose of description. When we wish to describe something or tell what it is like, we use the sentence with an adjectival predicate. When we ask "how is this blackboard" (这个黑板怎么样), we may answer:

13. 这个　黑板　很　大.
Zhèigè　hēibǎn　hěn　dà.
This blackboard is very big.

14. 这个　黑板　不　大.
Zhèigè　hēibǎn　bú　dà.
This blackboard is not big.

Or we may use other adjectives, such as 新, 旧, 長, 短, 小 and so on to describe the quality or shape of the blackboard.

On the other hand, the sentence with a substantive predicate (2) is used to judge of or explain something. When we ask "what blackboard" (什么黑板), "whose blackboard" (誰的黑板), "what kind of blackboard" (哪种黑板), "of what shape is the blackboard" (什么样的黑板) and so forth, then we have to use the sentence with a substantive predicate (2) in our answers.

Therefore, we may reach the conclusion that whenever we wish to describe the person or thing denoted by the subject, we use the sentence with an adjectival predicate, and whenever we wish to tell the kind of person or thing denoted by the subject, we use the sentence with a substantive predicate (2).

課文　Kèwén　Text

I

SIDE FIVE, BAND TWO

(a₁) 先生、学生　都　有　画报　吗?
Xiānshēng、xuéshēng dōu yǒu huàbào må?

Do the teacher and the student (both) have picture news magazines?

(b₁) 不, 学生　有　画报, 先生　没　有
Bù, xuéshēng yǒu huàbào, xiānshēng méi yǒu

画报. 先生　只　有　杂誌.
huàbào. Xiānshēng zhǐ yǒu zázhì.

No, the student has a picture news magazine, but the teacher doesn't. The teacher only has a magazine.

(a₂) 画报、杂誌　都　是　新的　吗?
Huàbào、 zázhì dōu shì xīndě må?

Are the picture news magazine and the magazine new ones?

(b₂) 是, 画报、杂誌　都　是　新的.
Shì, huàbào、 zázhì dōu shì xīndě.

Yes, they are.

II

(a₃) 这 是 不 是 铅笔？
Zhèi shì bú shì qiānbǐ?

Is this a pencil?

(b₃) 这 是 铅笔.
Zhèi shì qiānbǐ.

Yes.

(a₄) 那 也 是 铅笔 吗？
Nèi yě shì qiānbǐ må?

Is that a pencil too?

(b₄) 对 了, 那 也 是 铅笔.
Duì lě, nèi yě shì qiānbǐ.

That's right, it is.

(a₅) 这枝 铅笔 和 那枝 铅笔 都 是
Zhèizhī qiānbǐ hé nèizhī qiānbǐ dōu shì

你的 吗？
nǐdě må?

Are this pencil and that one yours?

(b₅) 不, 短的 是 我的, 長的 是 我
Bù, duǎndě shì wǒdě, chángdě shì wǒ

朋友的.
péngyǒudě.

No, the short one is mine and the long one is my friend's.

III

(a₆) 您 工作 不 工作？
Nín gōngzuò bù gōngzuò?

Do you (formal) work (not work)?

(b₆) 不 工作, 我 学习. 您也 学习 吗?
Bù gōngzuò, wǒ xuéxí. Nín yě xuéxí ma?
No, I study. Do you study too?

(a₇) 我 不 学习, 我 工作. 我 教 中文.
Wǒ bù xuéxí, wǒ gōngzuò. Wǒ jiāo zhōngwén.
No, I work. I teach Chinese.

(b₇) 您的 学生 多 不 多?
Nínde xuéshēng duō bù duō?
Do you (formal) have many students?

(a₈) 我的 学生 不 少.
Wǒde xuéshēng bù shǎo.
I have not a few students. (LIT.: My students are not few.)

(b₈) 您 教 俄文 不 教?
Nín jiāo èwén bù jiāo?
Do you teach Russian?

(a₉) 不 教, 我 不 会 俄文.
Bù jiāo, wǒ bú huì èwén.
No, I don't know Russian.

IV

(a₁₀) 你 有 本子 没 有?
Nǐ yǒu běnzǐ méi yǒu?
Do you have a notebook?

(b₁₀) 没 有, 我 有 纸, 没 有 本子.
Méi yǒu, wǒ yǒu zhǐ, méi yǒu běnzǐ.
No, I have paper; I do not have a notebook.

(a₁₁) 他 有 本子 没 有?
Tā yǒu běnzǐ méi yǒu?
Does he have a notebook?

(b₁₁) 他　有　本子,　也　有　紙.
Tā　yǒu　běnzǐ,　yě　yǒu　zhǐ.

He has a notebook and paper too.

(a₁₂) 这張　紙　是　干淨的　不　是?
Zhèizhāng　zhǐ　shì　gānjìngdě　bú　shì?

Is this sheet of paper a clean one?

(b₁₂) 是　干淨的,　这張　紙　很　干淨.
Shì　gānjìngdě,　zhèizhāng　zhǐ　hěn　gānjìng.

Yes, this sheet of paper is (very) clean.

Lesson 19

生詞 Shēngcí New Words

SIDE FIVE, BAND THREE

1.	誰	(代)	shéi	who
2.	什么	(代)	shénmǒ	what
3.	哪	(代)	něi	which
4.	怎么样	(代)	zěnmǒyàng	how (is it)
5.	叫	(动)	jiào	to call, to be called
6.	名字	(名)	míngzî	name
7.	些	(量)	xiē	some
8.	懂	(动)	dǒng	to understand
9.	学	(动)	xué	to learn, to study
10.	国	(名)	guó	country
11.	苏联	(名)	Sūlián	the Soviet Union
12.	知道	(动)	zhīdǎo	to know
13.	人民	(名)	rénmín	people
14.	同屋	(名)	tóngwū	roommate

語法 Yǔfǎ Grammar

19.1 The Interrogative Sentence (3) In the previous lessons, we have learned two kinds of interrogative sentences (13.3, 15.3). Here, we will deal with the third kind of interrogative sentence, made by using interrogative pronouns. e. g.

1. 他　是　誰?
   Tā　shì　shéi?
   Who is he? (LIT.: He is who?)

2. 他　是　先生.
   Tā　shì　xiānshěng.
   He is a teacher.

3. 这　是　什么?
   Zhèi　shì　shénmǒ?
   What is this? (LIT.: This is what?)

4. 这　是　画报.
   Zhèi　shì　huàbào.
   This is a picture news magazine.

5. 哪枝　鉛笔　短?
   Něizhī　qiānbǐ　duǎn?
   Which pencil is short?

6. 这枝　鉛笔　短.
   Zhèizhī　qiānbǐ　duǎn.
   This pencil is short.

7. 那本　杂誌　怎么样?
   Nèiběn　zázhì　zěnmǒyàng?
   How is that magazine?

8. 那本　杂誌　很　好.
   Nèiběn　zázhì　hěn　hǎo.
   That magazine is very good.

In the above, 誰, 什么, 哪, and 怎么样, are all interrogative pronouns.

There are two points to be noticed, when we use this kind of interrogative sentence:

(1) The question is asked by using the interrogative pronoun in the sentence, so the interrogative pronoun has to be placed where an answer is expected. e. g.

9. 誰　教　你們　中文?
Shéi jiāo nǐmen zhōngwén?
Who teaches you (plural) Chinese?

10. 那个　先生　教　我們　中文.
Nèige xiānshěng jiāo wǒmen zhōngwén.
That teacher teaches us Chinese.

11. 他　教　誰　中文?
Tā jiāo shéi zhōngwén?
Whom does he teach Chinese?

12. 他　教　我們　中文.
Tā jiāo wǒmen zhōngwén.
He teaches us Chinese.

The questions appear in different places in the above two examples, and the same word 誰 is used in two different positions; in the first sentence, it is used as subject, and in the second, it is used as object. Other examples are:

13. 你　看　哪本　画报?
Nǐ kàn něiběn huàbào?
Which picture news magazine do you read?

14. 我　看　这本　画报.
Wǒ kàn zhèiběn huàbào.
I read this picture news magazine.

15. 哪本　画报　有意思?
Něiběn huàbào yǒuyìsi?
Which picture news magazine is interesting?

16. 这本　画报　有意思.
Zhèiběn huàbào yǒuyìsi.
This picture news magazine is interesting.

For the same reasons, the same word 哪 is used as adjective modifier of the object and then as adjective modifier of the subject.

(2) The interrogative word itself forms an interrogative sentence; so there is no need to put the word 嗎 at the end of the sentence in which an interrogative pronoun has already been used.

19.2 The Substantive Sentence with the Verb 叫 There is one kind of sentence in which the verb of the predicate is 叫. The predicate of such kind of sentence is used mainly to tell the name of the person or thing denoted by the subject. e. g.

17. 这　叫　什么?
Zhèi　jiào　shénmǒ?
What is this called?

18. 这　叫　椅子.
Zhèi　jiào　yǐzi.
This is called a chair.

19. 他　叫　什么　名字?
Tā　jiào　shénmǒ　míngzi?
What is his name? (LIT.: He is called what name?)

20. 他　叫　張友文.
Tā　jiào　Zhāngyǒuwén.
He is called Chāng Yǒu-wén.

This kind of sentence is also called the sentence with a substantive predicate. Here the verb 叫 is a special verb, the same in nature and function as the copula 是. Hence, the element following 叫 is not an object, but a substantive predicate.

Note: 什么 in example 19 is used as adjective modifier, and different in use from 什么 in example 17. It is very common to use it as an adjective modifier.

19.3 一些　些 is a measure word used to express some quantity or number. e. g.

21. 我　有　一些　杂誌.
Wǒ　yǒu　yìxiē　zázhì.
I have some magazines.

22. 他　懂　一些　中文.
Tā　dǒng　yìxiē　zhōngwén.

He understands some Chinese.

The nouns following 一些 may be nouns denoting countable things (such as 杂誌), or nouns denoting uncountable things (such as 中文).

Except when used at the beginning of a sentence, 一 of 一些 may be omitted. e. g.

23. 他　有　(一)些　中国　朋友.
Tā　yǒu　(yì)xiē　Zhōngguó　péngyǒu.

He has some Chinese friends.

24. 先生　給　我　(一)些　杂誌.
Xiānshěng　gěi　wǒ　(yì)xiē　zázhì.

The teacher gives me some magazines.

When it is used together with 这, 那 and 哪, 一 is always omitted. Indeed we may say 这些, 那些, and 哪些 are the plural forms of 这, 那 and 哪. e. g.

25. 这些　鉛笔　都　是　短的.
Zhèixiē　qiānbǐ　dōu　shì　duǎndè.

These pencils are all short ones.

26. 哪些　桌子　干淨?
Něixiē　zhuōzi　gānjǐng?

Which tables are clean?

27. 那些　桌子　干淨.
Nèixiē　zhuōzi　gānjǐng.

Those tables are clean.

課文 Kèwén Text

SIDE FIVE, BAND THREE

I

(a₁) 那个 同志 是 誰?
Nèigè tóngzhì shì shéi?

Who is that comrade?

(b₁) 她 是 我的 朋友.
Tā shì wǒdě péngyǒu.

She is my friend.

(a₂) 哪个 先生 教 她?
Něigè xiānshěng jiāo tā?

Which teacher is her instructor?

(b₂) 張 先生 教 她.
Zhāng xiānshěng jiāo tā.

Her instructor is Mr. Chang.

(a₃) 她 学 什么?
Tā xué shénmǒ?

What does she study?

(b₃) 她 学 中文.
Tā xué zhōngwén.

She studies Chinese.

(a₄) 她 是 哪国 人?
Tā shì něiguó rén?

Where is she from?

(b₄) 她 是 苏联 人.
Tā shì Sūlián rén.

She is from the Soviet Union.

(a₅)   她　叫　什么　名字?
　　　　Tā　jiào　shénmò　míngzì?
　　　　What is her name?

(b₅)   我　不　知道.
　　　　Wǒ　bù　zhīdào.
　　　　I don't know.

(a₆)   她的　中文　怎么样?
　　　　Tādě　zhōngwén　zěnmòyàng?
　　　　How is her Chinese?

(b₆)   不　很　好,　懂　一些.
　　　　Bù　hěn　hǎo,　dǒng　yìxiē.
　　　　Not very good; she understands a little.

II

(a₇)   这本　書　是　誰的?
　　　　Zhèiběn　shū　shì　shéidě?
　　　　Whose book is this?

(b₇)   这本　書　是　我的.
　　　　Zhèiběn　shū　shì　wǒdě.
　　　　This book is mine.

(a₈)   这　是　一本　什么　書?
　　　　Zhèi　shì　yìběn　shénmò　shū?
　　　　What kind of book is this?

(b₈)   这　是　一本　中文　書.
　　　　Zhèi　shì　yìběn　zhōngwén　shū.
　　　　This is a Chinese book.

(a₉)　这　叫　什么?
Zhèi　jiào　shénmɔ?
What is this called?

(b₉)　这　叫　画报.
Zhèi　jiào　huàbào.
This is called a picture news magazine.

(a₁₀)　这　是　什么　画报?
Zhèi　shì　shénmɔ　huàbào?
What picture news magazine is this?

(b₁₀)　这　是　"人民　画报".
Zhèi　shì　"Rénmín　Huàbào".
This is "The People's Picture Magazine."

(a₁₁)　"人民　画报"　怎么样?
"Rénmín　Huàbào"　zěnmɔyàng?
How is "The People's Picture Magazine?"

(b₁₁)　很　有意思.
Hěn　yǒuyìsì.
Very interesting.

(a₁₂)　那些　是　什么?
Nèixiē　shì　shénmɔ?
What are those?

(b₁₂)　哪些?　这些　都　是　旧　杂誌.
Něixiē?　Zhèixiē　dōu　shì　jiù　zázhì.
Which ones? These are all old magazines.

(a₁₃)　那些　旧　杂誌　都　怎么样?
Nèixiē　jiù　zázhì　dōu　zěnmɔyàng?
How are those old magazines?

(b₁₈) 我 也 不 知道. 这些 杂誌 都
Wǒ　yě　bù　zhīdào.　Zhèixiē　zázhì　dōu

不 是 我的. 都 是 我 同屋
bú　shì　wǒdė.　Dōu　shì　wǒ　tóngwū-

的.
dė.

I don't know myself. These magazines aren't mine.
They are my roommate's.

課外練習　Kèwài liànxí　Home Work

1) Answer the following questions (Names of persons and coun-
tries may be written in phonetic spellings.):

(1) 你的　同屋　叫　什么　名字?

(2) 你　知道　他的　中国　名字　嗎?

(3) 这个　同志　是　哪国　人?

(4) 他　懂　不　懂　俄文?

2) Make sentences with each of the following words and word
combinations:

(5) 誰的

(6) 哪些

(7) 什么

(8) 怎么样

汉字表　Hànzì biǎo　Chinese Characters

1	誰							
2	什	亻						
		十						
3	么	丿	么					
4	哪	口						
		那						
5	怎	乍						
		心						
6	样	木						
		羊（丶　丷　丷　羊）						
7	叫	口						
		丩（乚　丩）						
8	名	夕						
		口						
9	字							
10	些	丨	𠂉	止	此	此	些	些
11	懂	忄						
		董	艹					
			重（丿　二　𠂇　𠚕　重　重）					

12	苏	比
		办（力 力 办）
13	联	耳
		关（丶 ヽ 丷 半 关 关）
14	知	
15	道	
16	民	ㄱ ㄱ ㄹ ㄹ 民
17	屋	尸
		至（一 云 至）

Lesson 20

生詞 Shēngcí New Words

1. 积極 (形) jījí enthusiastic, active
2. 努力 (形) nǔlì diligent, strenuous
3. 跟 (介) gēn with, after
4. 从 (介) cóng from
5. 学校 (名) xuéxiào school
6. 一起 (副) yìqǐ together
7. 那兒(那里) (代) nàr (nàlǐ) there
8. 这兒(这里) (代) zhèr(zhèlǐ) here
9. 去 (动) qù to go
10. 地 (助) dē (a structural particle)
11. 高兴 (形) gāoxìng glad, happy
12. 喜欢 (动) xǐhuǎn to like, to be fond of
13. 电影 (名) diànyǐng film, moving picture
14. 哪兒(哪里) (代) nǎr (nǎlǐ) where

語法 Yǔfǎ Grammar

20.1 **The Adverbial Modifier**   The adverbial modifier is an element used to modify the verb or the adjective. Besides adverbs, there are many words of other parts of speech and constructions that can function as adverbial modifiers. In this lesson, only adjectives and prepositional constructions are introduced as adverbial modifiers.

(1) Adjectives Used as Adverbial Modifiers   Adjectives are not only used as adjective modifiers and predicates, but also as adverbial modifiers. e. g.

1. 这个　同志　<u>积極</u>　工作.
Zhèige tóngzhì jījí gōngzuò.
This comrade works enthusiastically.

2. 他的　同屋　<u>努力</u>　学習.
Tāde tóngwū nǔlì xuéxí.
His roommate studies diligently.

Here, the adjectives 积極 and 努力 are used as adverbial modifiers to 工作 and 学習. Adverbial modifiers are always put before the central words or the words modified.

(2) The Prepositional Construction (Phrase) Used as Adverbial Modifier   A preposition always carries its own object in a prepositional construction. It can be used either as adjective modifier or as adverbial modifier. When it is used as adverbial modifier, it has to be placed before the central word. e. g.

3. 我　朋友　<u>跟</u>　我　很　好.
Wǒ péngyǒu gēn wǒ hěn hǎo.
My friend is very good to me.

4. 那个　同志　<u>从　学校</u>　来.
Nèige tóngzhì cóng xuéxiào lái.
That comrade is coming (OR: comes) from school.

跟 and 从 are prepositions, and 跟我 and 从学校 are prepositional constructions. 跟我 modifies the adjective 好, and 从学校 modifies the verb 来.

In Chinese, there are some prepositions that are rather difficult to use properly. For the present, let us discuss only the following two prepositions 跟 and 从:

(1) 跟 It is commonly used in two ways. It may be used with the meaning of "to" or "with," pointing out the object to which action or feeling is directed. See example 3. It may also be used with the meaning of "together with." e. g.

5. 她 跟 我 看 一張 报.
　Tā　gēn　wǒ　kàn　yìzhāng　bào.
She is reading a newspaper (together) with me. (LIT.: She with me reads one sheet newspaper.)

The adverb 一起 is often used together with the prepositional construction composed of 跟. e. g.

6. 我 朋友 跟 我 一起 学習.
　Wǒ　péngyǒu　gēn　wǒ　yìqǐ　xuéxí.
My friend studies (together) with me.

(2) 从 从 denotes a starting point, its object may be a word or word group of time or of place. 学校 in example 4 is a word denoting place. (The words expressing time will be introduced afterwards.) When such a construction is used to represent place, the object must be a noun or pronoun denoting place. e. g.

7. 先生 从 学校 来.
　Xiānshěng　cóng　xuéxiào　lái.
The teacher comes from school.

8. 他 从 那兒 来.
　Tā　cóng　nàr　lái.
He is coming from there.

When the starting point of an action is represented by a person or persons, we have to change the noun or pronoun denoting persons into a word for place by adding 这兒 or 那兒. e. g.

9. 他　从　朋友　那兒　来.
   Tā　cóng　péngyǒu　nàr　lái.

   He is coming from (seeing) his friend (OR: from his
   friend's place). (LIT.: He from friend there comes.)

10. 我　从　你　这兒　去.
    Wǒ　cóng　nǐ　zhèr　qù.

    I am going (away) from you. (LIT.: I from you here
    go.)

20.2 The Repetition of Adjectives　In Chinese, adjectives
can be repeated by reduplicating the syllable:

11. 好　——→　好好兒
    hǎo　——→　hǎohāor
    good　　　very good

12. 干淨　——→　干干淨淨
    gānjìng　——→　gāngānjìngjìng
    clean　　　very clean

When a monosyllabic adjective is reduplicated, the second
syllable is always pronounced in the 1st tone with the retroflex
"兒". When a dissyllabic adjective is reduplicated, the final
syllable is always stressed.

The reduplicated adjective has the function of emphasizing
the quality expressed by that adjective. It can be used either
as adjective modifier or as adverbial modifier. As adverbial
modifier, it is in general followed by the structural particle 地
(also written as 的) to join it with the central word. e. g.

13. 我們　都　好好兒地　学習.
    Wǒmen　dōu　hǎohāorde　xuéxí.
    We all study very well.

14. 同志們　都　高高兴兴地　工作.
    Tóngzhìmen　dōu　gāogāoxìngxìngde　gōngzuò.
    All the comrades work very gladly.

課文 Kèwén Text

SIDE FIVE, BAND FOUR

I

(a₁) 那个 新 同志 是 誰?
Nèigě xīn tóngzhì shì shéi?

Who is that new comrade?

(b₁) 那个 新 同志 是 我的 朋友.
Nèigě xīn tóngzhì shì wǒdě péngyǒu.

他的 名字 叫 張友文.
Tādě míngzì jiào Zhāngyǒuwén.

That new comrade is my friend. His name is Chāng Yǒu-wén.

(a₂) 那个 新 同志 怎么样?
Nèigě xīn tóngzhì zěnmǒyàng?

How is that new comrade?

(b₂) 很 好, 很 积极. 他 会 中文, 也
Hěn hǎo, hěn jījí. Tā huì zhōngwén, yě

懂 俄文. 他 积极地 工作, 我們
dǒng èwén. Tā jījídě gōngzuò, wǒmén

都 喜欢 他.
dōu xǐhuān tā.

Very good, very enthusiastic. He knows Chinese and understands Russian too. He works enthusiastically and we all like him.

II

(a₃) 这个 学生 学 什么?
Zhèigě xuéshēng xué shénmǒ?

What does this student study?

(b₃) 他 学 中文.
Tā xué zhōngwén.

He studies Chinese.

(a₄) 他　跟　你　一起　学习　吗?
Tā　gēn　nǐ　yìqǐ　xuéxí　må?
Does he study together with you?

(b₄) 对了,　我們　一起　学习,　我們　很
Duìlė,　wǒmėn　yìqǐ　xuéxí,　wǒmėn　hěn
努力地　学习,　我們　都　高高兴兴
nǔlìdė　xuéxí,　wǒmėn　dōu　gāogåoxìngxìng-
地　学习.
dė　xuéxí.
That's right, we study together; we study very diligently; we both study very gladly.

III

(a₅) 您　看　电影　不　看?
Nín　kàn　diànyǐng　bú　kàn?
Are you (formal) going to see the film?

(b₅) 看.
Kàn.
Yes.

(a₆) 您　从　哪兒　去?
Nín　cóng　nǎr　qù?
Where are you going from?

(b₆) 我　从　学校　去,　你　也　从　学校
Wǒ　cóng　xuéxiào　qù,　nǐ　yě　cóng　xuéxiào
去　吗?
qù　må?
I am going from school; are you going from school
too?

(a₇) 不,　我　从　朋友　那兒　去.
Bù,　wǒ　cóng　péngyǒu　nàr　qù.
No, I'm going from my friend's place.

課外練習 Kèwài liànxí Home Work

Translate the following English into Chinese:
1) Where have you come from?
   I have come from teacher Chang's place.
2) With whom do you study?
   I study with him.
3) What do you study together?
   We study Chinese and Russian together.
4) Will you see the film (or the moving picture)?
   Yes. we will. It is very interesting.

汉字表 Hànzì biǎo Chinese Characters

1	积	禾	
		只	
2	極	木	
		亟（一 丆 了 丆 亟 亟）	
3	努	奴	女
			又
		力	
4	力		
5	跟		
6	从	人	
		人	
7	校	木	
		交（丶 亠 六 交 交）	

8	起	走 (土 𡳿 𡳿 𡳿 走 走)	
		巳 (𠃍 コ 巳)	
9	兒		
10	里	日 旦 甲 里	
11	去		
12	地	土	
		也	
13	高	、 亠 亠 亠 高 高	
14	兴	、 ⺍ ⺍ 丷 兴	
15	喜	土 吉 吉 吉 喜 喜	
16	欢	又	
		欠	
17	电	日 电	
18	影	景	日
			京
		彡 (丿 彡 彡)	

Lesson 21

生詞 Shēngcí New Words

SIDE FIVE, BAND FIVE

1.	念	(动)	niàn	to read
2.	得	(助)	dē	(a structural particle)
3.	早	(形)	zǎo	early
4.	快	(形)	kuài	quick, fast
5.	写	(动)	xiě	to write
6.	汉字	(名)	hànzì	Chinese character
7.	晚	(形)	wǎn	late
8.	慢	(形)	màn	slow
9.	常常	(副)	chángcháng	often
10.	說(話)	(动)	shuō (huà)	to speak
11.	話	(名)	huà	words, speech
12.	太	(副)	tài	too
13.	跳(舞)	(动)	tiào (wǔ)	to dance
14.	一定	(副)	yídìng	certainly
15.	唱(歌兒)	(动)	chàng (gēr)	to sing (song)
16.	歌兒	(名)	gēr	song

語法 Yǔfǎ Grammar

21.1 **The Verb-Object Construction** The construction composed of a verb and an object is termed a verb-object construction. Today we shall learn a special kind of verb-object construction. It has two characteristic features:

(1) So far as its meaning is concerned, it represents a single idea equivalent to a verb without object in English. e.g.

1. 我　念　書.
   Wǒ　niàn　shū.

   I study. (LIT.: I read book.)

2. 先生　教　書.
   Xiānshêng jiāo　shū.

   The teacher teaches. (LIT.: Teacher teaches book.)

Structurally speaking, 念書 and 教書 are two verb-object constructions, they are equivalent to two simple verbs "to study" and "to teach" in English. Here 書 is the object, but it is so habitually used that it has already lost the concrete meaning of "book". Yet, in the above examples, the word 書 is necessary, because in Chinese we are not accustomed to say 我念 and 先生教. Without 書 the meaning of the sentence is incomplete.

(2) So far as its construction is concerned, it is a combination of a verb and its object. It is the same in use as the general verb-object constructions. We must never use another object after such a construction. If another object is required, the habitually used object has to be omitted. e. g.

3. 我　念　中文.
   Wǒ　niàn　zhōngwén.

   I read Chinese.

4. 先生　教　中文.
   Xiānshêng jiāo　zhōngwén.

   The teacher teaches Chinese.

Then, we can't say 念書中文 or 教書中文.

21.2 The Complement of Degree　A word or words placed after a verb or adjective to tell something more about the action of the verb or the quality of the adjective are called a complementary element, and the verb or adjective is called the central word. The adjective modifier or the adverbial modifier is placed before the central word, while the complementary element is placed after the central word. There are several kinds of complementary element, here let us take a look at the complement of degree. Whenever we wish to describe emphatically the degree or extent (or result) an action has reached, we use the complement of degree. The action is often already completed (or taken for granted that it is completed), or it is habitually frequent, or has gained a certain level or result. e. g.

5. 他　来得　早.
　　Tā　láidê　zǎo.
　　He arrives early.

6. 我　念得　快.
　　Wǒ　niàndê　kuài.
　　I read quickly.

早 is used to complete 来, and 快 is used to complete 念.

21.3 Rules Concerning the Complement of Degree

(1) The main feature of the complement of degree is that between the verb and the complement there is a structural particle 得 used as connective. (得 and 的 have the same pronunciation, may be used interchangeably.)

(2) The complement of degree is generally composed of an adjective. But in a complicated sentence, it is very common to use a complicated construction as the complement of degree.

(3) If there is an object after the verb, we have to reduplicate the verb and place the complement after the second form of the verb. e. g.

7. 他　学　中文　学得　快.
　　Tā　xué　zhōngwén　xuédê　kuài.
　　He learns Chinese quickly. (= As for learning Chinese, he learns it quickly.)

8. 先生　教　中文　教得　好.
Xiānshěng jiāo zhōngwén jiāodě hǎo.
The teacher teaches Chinese well.

Hence, in the special kind of verb-object constructions mentioned above, we have to reduplicate the verb too. e. g.

9. 他　念　書　念得　快.
Tā niàn shū niàndě kuài.
He studies quickly.

10. 先生　教　書　教得　好.
Xiānshěng jiāo shū jiāodě hǎo.
The teacher teaches well.

(4) In the sentence containing a complement of degree, the complement is very important. The verb or verbal construction standing before it seems merely the subject of the sentence. Therefore:

(a) In the negative sentence, the negative adverb 不 is not placed before the verb (or adjective) but before the complement. e. g.

11. 他　来得　不　早.
Tā láidě bù zǎo.
He does not come early.

12. 我　写　汉字　写得　不　快.
Wǒ xiě hànzì xiědě bú kuài.
I don't write Chinese characters quickly. (= As for writing Chinese characters, I don't write them quickly.)

We do not often use a word in the negative form as complement; instead, we use its antonym. e. g.

13. 他　来得　晚.
Tā láidě wǎn.
He comes late.

14. 我　写　汉字　写得　慢.
    Wǒ　xiě　hànzì　xiědě　màn.
    I write Chinese characters slowly.

(b) In the alternative interrogative sentence, we give both the affirmative and the negative forms of the complement but not those of the verb. e. g.

15. 他　来得　晚　不　晚?
    Tā　láidě　wǎn　bù　wǎn?
    Does he come late?

16. 他　学　中文　学得　快　不　快?
    Tā　xué　zhōngwén　xuédě　kuài　bú　kuài?
    Does he learn Chinese quickly?

課文　Kèwén　Text

SIDE FIVE, BAND FIVE

I

1. 先生　常常　来得　很　早.
   Xiānshěng　chángcháng　láidě　hěn　zǎo.
   The teacher often comes very early.

2. 学生　也　来得　很　早.
   Xuéshěng　yě　láidě　hěn　zǎo.
   The student also comes very early.

3. 先生　說　話　說得　不　太　快.
   Xiānshěng　shuō　huà　shuōdě　bú　tài　kuài.
   The teacher does not speak too quickly.

4. 那些　学生　跳　舞　跳得　很　高兴.
   Nèixiē　xuéshěng　tiào　wǔ　tiàodě　hěn　gāoxìng.
   Those students enjoy dancing very much.

5. 張　同志　看　中文　报　一定　看得
Zhāng　tóngzhì　kàn　zhōngwén　bào　yídìng　kàndê

很　快.
hěn　kuài.

Comrade Chāng certainly reads Chinese newspapers
very quickly.

6. 他　懂　俄文,　他　説　俄文　説得
Tā　dǒng　èwén,　tā　shuō　èwén　shuōdê

很　好.
hěn　hǎo.

He understands Russian and speaks Russian well.

II

(a₁) 你們　学習得　怎么样?
Nǐmên　xuéxídê　zěnmôyàng?

How do you study?

(b₁) 我　学習得　不　太　好,　張　同志
Wǒ　xuéxídê　bú　tài　hǎo,　Zhāng　tóngzhì

学習得　很　好.
xuéxídê　hěn　hǎo.

I don't study too well, but Comrade Chāng studies
well.

(a₂) 你們　写　汉字　嗎?
Nǐmên　xiě　hànzì　mâ?

Do you write Chinese characters?

(b₂) 写　汉字.　我們　都　写得　很　慢.
Xiě　hànzì.　Wǒmên　dōu　xiědê　hěn　màn.

Yes. We all write them very slowly.

(a₃) 張　同志　也　寫得　很　慢　嗎?
Zhāng tóngzhì yě xiědê hěn màn mâ?
Does Comrade Chāng also write them very slowly?

(b₃) 不,　張　同志　寫得　很　快.
Bù, Zhāng tóngzhì xiědê hěn kuài.
No, Comrade Chāng writes them very quickly.

(a₄) 你們　喜欢　唱　歌兒　不　喜欢?
Nǐmên xǐhuân chàng gēr bù xǐhuân?
Do you like to sing?

(b₄) 喜欢. 我們　常常　跟　中国　朋友
Xǐhuân. Wǒmên chángcháng gēn Zhōngguó péngyôu

一起　唱　歌兒. 中国　朋友　教
yìqǐ chàng gēr. Zhōngguó péngyôu jiāo

我們　中国　歌兒. 我們　跟　中国
wǒmên Zhōngguó gēr. Wǒmên gēn Zhōngguó

朋友　一起　唱得　很　高兴.
péngyôu yìqǐ chàngdê hěn gāoxìng.

We do. We often sing together with Chinese friends.
Our Chinese friends teach us Chinese songs. We enjoy
singing together with our Chinese friends.

課外練習　Kèwài liànxi　Home Work

1) Translate the following into Chinese:
(1) This comrade always comes very early.
(2) The students in our school learn Russian very rapidly.
(3) I read Chinese books very slowly.

2) Complete the following sentences with complements of degree:

(4) 她 跳 舞 _____.

(5) 那些 中国 学生 说 俄文 _____.

(6) 先生 写 我的 名字 _____

_____.

(7) 努力的 学生 一定 学习 _____

_____.

(8) 我的 同屋 唱 中国 歌兒 ____

_____.

汉字表 Hànzì biǎo Chinese Characters

1	念	今 (人 仝 今)
		心
2	得	
3	早	日
		十
4	快	
5	写	宀 (丶 宀)
		与 (一 与 与)
6	汉	

7	晚	日（丨 𠃌 月 日）	
		免（丿 ⺈ ⺈ 㲋 㲋 㲋 免）	
8	慢		
9	常	尚	⺌冖（丨 丶 ⺌ ⺌冖）
			口
		巾（丨 冂 巾）	
10	說	言	
		兑（丶 丷 𠮛 兑）	
11	話	言	
		舌（丿 二 千 舌）	
12	太	大 太	
13	跳	𧾷	
		兆（丿 ⺦ ⺦ 兆 兆 兆）	
14	舞	無（丿 𠂉 𠂉 午 午 無 無 無）	
		舛（夕 夕 夕 夕 舛）	
15	定	宀	
		疋	
16	唱		
17	歌	哥	可
			可
		欠	

Lesson 22

生詞 Shēngcí New Words

1. 二	(数)	èr	two
2. 四	(数)	sì	four
3. 五	(数)	wǔ	five
4. 六	(数)	liù	six
5. 七	(数)	qī	seven
6. 八	(数)	bā	eight
7. 九	(数)	jiǔ	nine
8. 十	(数)	shí	ten
9. 两	(数)	liǎng	two
10. 几	(数)	jǐ	how many, several, a few
11. 多少	(数)	duōshǎo	how many, how much
12. 半	(数)	bàn	half
13. 年	(名)	nián	year
14. 練習	(名、动)	liànxí	exercise, to exercise, to practise

語法 Yǔfǎ Grammar

22.1 **The Enumeration of Cardinal Numerals from One to Ninety-nine** In Chinese, the decimal system is used for counting numbers. Besides the numerals 一, 二, 三, 四, 五, 六, 七, 八, 九 and 十, are the numerals 十一, 十二 etc. The numerals from 11 to 99 are formed by the following three methods:

(1) From eleven to nineteen the numerals are formed by addition. For example: 11 is 10 plus 1; 19 is 10 plus 9.

(2) 20, 30, 40, 50, 60, 70, 80, 90 are formed by multiplication. For example: 30 is 10 multiplied by 3, 50 is 10 multiplied by 5.

(3) The numerals between the tens are formed first by multiplication, then by addition. For example: 22 is two tens plus 2, 78 is seven tens plus 8.

22.2 二 and 两   In Chinese, the numerals 二 and 两 denote the same number "two", but they are different in use:

(1) Before measure words we prefer 两 to 二. e. g.

1. 两个　朋友
liǎnggè　péngyǒu
two friends

2. 两张　桌子
liǎngzhāng　zhuōzǐ
two tables

There are a few exceptions, such as 二斤糖 (two catties of sugar) and 二年 (two years). Yet, even in such cases, we may use 两 instead of 二.

(2) If 2 comes at the end of a big number, we have to use 二 and never 两. e. g.

3. 十二个　学生
shíèrgè　xuéshēng
twelve students

4. 四十二把　椅子
sìshíèrbǎ　yǐzi
forty-two chairs

(3) "20" is only read as 二十, never as 两十.

22.3 几 and 多少   In asking about numbers or figures we use 几 and 多少; however, they are not always used interchangeably:

(1) 多少 may be used to ask about any number, big or small; while 几 is often used for the numbers from one to nine. For example:

5. 你　有　几本　"人民　画报"?
　　Nǐ　yǒu　jǐběn　"Rénmín　Huàbào"?

How many (copies of) "The People's Picture Magazine" do you have? (up to nine)

6. 你　有　多少本　"人民　画报"?
　　Nǐ　yǒu　duōshǎoběn　"Rénmín　Huàbào"?

How many (copies of) "The People's Picture Magazine" do you have? (any number)

Both sentences are questions about the number of pictorials. When the number of pictorials is less than ten, it is example 5; when the number of pictorials is indefinite, it is example 6. 几 is often used before 十. e. g.

7. 你　有　几十本　杂誌?
　　Nǐ　yǒu　jǐshíběn　zázhì?

How many magazines do you have? (multiples of ten)

8. 你　有　十几本　杂誌?
　　Nǐ　yǒu　shíjǐběn　zázhì?

How many magazines do you have? (between eleven and nineteen)

The expected answers will be 20, 30...or 90 to example **7**, and 11, 12...or 19 to example **8**.

(2) 多少 can be directly connected with a noun, while 几 must be followed by a measure word. e. g.

9. 这个　学校　有　多少(个)　先生?
　　Zhèige　xuéxiào　yǒu　duōshǎo(ge)　xiānshēng?

How many teachers are there in this school? (LIT.: This school has how many teachers?)

10. 那个　同志　有　几本　杂誌?
　　Nèige tóngzhì yǒu jǐběn zázhì?

How many magazines does that comrade have? (up to nine)

22.4 半　　It is a numeral. Be careful of the position of this numeral when it is used together with a measure word:

(1) When there is no numeral used together with 半, it can be directly placed before the measure word like the general numerals. e. g.

11. 半張　紙
　　bǎnzhāng zhǐ

half a sheet of paper

12. 半年
　　bànnián

half a year

(2) When the word 半 is used together with numerals, the integral numerals are put before the measure word, while the word 半 follows the measure word. e. g.

13. 兩張半　紙
　　liǎngzhāngbàn zhǐ

two and a half sheets of paper

14. 兩年半
　　liǎngniánbàn

two and a half years

課文　Kèwén Text

SIDE FIVE, BAND SIX

I

(a₁) 你　有　画报　嗎?
　　Nǐ yǒu huàbào mǎ?

Do you have a picture news magazine?

(b₁) 有， 我 有 中文 画报， 也 有
Yǒu, wǒ yǒu zhōngwén huàbào, yě yǒu

俄文 画报.
èwén huàbào.

Yes, I have a Chinese picture news magazine, and a Russian one also.

(a₂) 你 有 多少本 中文 画报?
Nǐ yǒu duōshǎoběn zhōngwén huàbào?

How many Chinese picture news magazines do you have?

(b₂) 我 有 十二本 中文 画报.
Wǒ yǒu shíèrběn zhōngwén huàbào.

I have twelve Chinese picture news magazines.

(a₃) 你 有 多少本 俄文 画报?
Nǐ yǒu duōshǎoběn èwén huàbào?

How many Russian picture news magazines do you have?

(b₃) 我的 俄文 画报 不 多, 只 有
Wǒdě èwén huàbào bù duō, zhǐ yǒu

三本.
sānběn.

I don't have many Russian picture news magazines, only three.

II

(a₄) 这个 学校 有 多少(个) 苏联
Zhèigě xuéxiào yǒu duōshǎo(gě) Sūlián

学生?
xuéshěng?

How many Soviet students are there in this school?

(b₄) 有 二十二个 苏联 学生.
Yǒu èrshíèrgě Sūlián xuéshěng.

There are twenty-two Soviet students.

(a₅) 他們 都 学 中文 嗎?
Tāmén dōu xué zhōngwén må?
Do they all study Chinese?

(b₅) 他們 都 学 中文.
Tāmén dōu xué zhōngwén.
Yes.

(a₆) 几个 先生 教 这些 学生?
Jǐgè xiānshēng jiāo zhèixiē xuéshēng?
How many teachers instruct these students?

(b₆) 两个 先生.
Liǎnggè xiānshēng.
Two teachers.

(a₇) 一个 先生 教 多少 学生?
Yígè xiānshēng jiāo duōshǎo xuéshēng?
How many students does one teacher instruct?

(b₇) 一个 先生 教 十一个 学生.
Yígè xiānshēng jiāo shíyīgè xuéshēng.
One teacher instructs eleven students.

III

(a₈) 你 有 几个 中国 朋友?
Nǐ yǒu jǐgè Zhōngguó péngyǒu?
How many Chinese friends do you have?

(b₈) 我 有 三个.
Wǒ yǒu sāngè.
I have three.

(a₉) 他們 唱 不 唱 苏联 歌兒?
Tāmén chàng bú chàng Sūlián gēr?
Do they sing Soviet songs?

(b₉) 唱, 他們 唱 苏联 歌兒.
Chàng, tāmên chàng Sūlián gēr.
Yes, they do.

(a₁₀) 他們 会 多少 苏联 歌兒?
Tāmên huì duōshảo Sūlián gēr?
How many Soviet songs do they know?

(b₁₀) 他們 会 很 多.
Tāmên huì hěn duō.
They know many.

(a₁₁) 你 会 中国 歌兒 嗎?
Nǐ huì Zhōngguó gēr mả?
Do you know Chinese songs?

(b₁₁) 会, 我 只 会 两个.
Huì, wǒ zhǐ huì liǎnggê.
Yes, (but) I know only two.

(a₁₂) 誰 教 你 中国 歌兒?
Shéi jiāo nǐ Zhōngguó gēr?
Who teaches you Chinese songs?

(b₁₂) 我的 中国 朋友.
Wǒdê Zhōngguó péngyǒu.
My Chinese friends.

(a₁₃) 你 常常 練習 嗎?
Nǐ chángcháng liànxí mả?
Do you practice often?

(b₁₃) 我 常常 練習.
Wǒ chángcháng liànxí.
Yes.

課外練習 Kèwài liànxí Home Work

1) Write out the following numbers in Chinese and phonetic spellings and give the tone-marks:

    (1) 16   (2) 32   (3) 95   (4) 40
    (5) 22   (6) 81   (7) 53   (8) 77

2) Copy the following sentences and change the numbers within parentheses into Chinese numerals:

    (9) 那 (2)枝 短 鉛笔 是 誰的?
    (10) 他 有 (52)本 杂誌.

3) Fill the blanks with 几 or 多少 and pay attention to the use of the measure word:

    (11) 他 会 ＿＿ 汉字?
    不 知道, 他 一定 会 很 多.
    (12) 那个 学生 有 ＿＿ 鋼笔?
    只 有 一枝.

汉字表 Hànzì biǎo Chinese Characters

1	二	一 二
2	四	丶 冂 冂 四 四
3	五	一 丁 互 五
4	六	丶 亠 六
5	七	一 七
6	八	
7	九	

8	十	
9	兩	一 一 丙 兩
10	几	
11	半	丶 丷 兰 半
12	年	ノ 乞 二 乍 年 年
13	練	糸
		柬(一 一 丂 両 両 両 車 東 柬)

Lesson 23

生詞 Shēngcí New Words
SIDE FIVE, BAND SEVEN

1.	在	(动) zài	to be on, in, at
2.	里边兒	(名) lǐbiānr	inside
3.	外边兒	(名) wàibiānr	outside
4.	上边兒	(名) shàngbiānr	above
5.	下边兒	(名) xiàbiānr	below, the following
6.	中間兒	(名) zhōngjiànr	middle
7.	前边兒	(名) qiánbiānr	front
8.	工厂	(名) gōngchǎng	factory
9.	后边兒	(名) hòubiānr	back, the following
10.	宿舍	(名) sùshè	dormitory, hostel
11.	作	(动) zuò	to do, to make, to work, to be
12.	地方	(名) dìfāng	place
13.	圖書館	(名) túshūguǎn	library
14.	礼堂	(名) lǐtáng	auditorium (hall)
15.	旁边兒	(名) pángbiānr	side, beside

語法 Yǔfǎ Grammar

23.1 在 在 is a verb and can be used as the chief element of a predicate. e. g.

1. 你 在 哪兒?
   Nǐ zài nǎr?
   Where are you? (LIT.: You are-at where?)

2. 我 在 学校.
   Wǒ zài xuéxiào.
   I am at school.

It can also be used as a preposition. If the object of 在 is composed of a word or word group of place, then this preposition and its object form a prepositional construction which is often used as adverbial modifier of place. e. g.

3. 我們 在 中国 学習,
   Wǒmen zài Zhōngguó xuéxí.
   We are studying in China.

4. 先生 在 这兒 工作.
   Xiānshēng zài zhèr gōngzuò.
   The teacher works here (LIT.: at here).

Whether the word 在 is used as a verb or a preposition, its object is in general a noun or pronoun denoting place. If the noun or pronoun denotes a person, then just as in the case of 从, 这兒 and 那兒 must be used to change this object into one denoting place. e. g.

5. 我的 練習 本子 在 先生 那兒.
   Wǒde liànxí běnzi zài xiānshēng nàr.
   My exercise notebook is at the teacher's place (LIT.: at teacher there).

6. 中国 朋友 在 我們 这兒 看 画报.
   Zhōngguó péngyǒu zài wǒmen zhèr kàn huàbào.
   (Our) Chinese friend is reading a picture news magazine (here) at our place.

Of course, the word 在 may be followed by a noun denoting time.

23.2 **Nouns of Locality**   Some nouns are used exclusively to indicate locality, e. g. 里边兒, 外边兒, 上边兒, 下边兒, 中間兒 etc. Like other nouns, a noun of locality can be used as subject. e. g.

7. 里边兒　很　干淨.
　　Lǐbiānr　hěn　gānjǐng.
　　It is very clean inside. (LIT.: Inside very clean.)

It can be used as object. e. g.

8. 我　在　外边兒.
　　Wǒ　zài　wàibiānr.
　　I am outside.

It can also be used as adjective modifier. e. g.

9. 上边兒的　杂誌　是　新的.
　　Shàngbiānrdê　zázhì　shì　xīndê.
　　The magazine on top is a new one.

10. 我　不　看　下边兒的　旧　杂誌.
　　Wǒ　bú　kàn　xiàbiānrdê　jiù　zázhì.
　　I do not read the old magazine at the bottom.

As a central word, it can also be modified by a noun or a pronoun. e. g.

11. 那張　桌子　在　两把　椅子　中間兒.
　　Nèizhāng　zhuōzǐ　zài　liǎngbǎ　yǐzǐ　zhōngjiànr.
　　That table is between the two chairs. (LIT.: That table is at the two chairs' middle.)

12. 先生　在　我們　前边兒.
　　Xiānshêng　zài　wǒmên　qiánbiānr.
　　The teacher is in front of us.

In the word combinations of 两把椅子中間兒 and of 我們前边兒, the word 的 is often understood and omitted.

When 上边兒 and 里边兒 are used after nouns, we often omit the word 边兒. e. g.

13. 練習　本子　在　桌子上.
　　Liànxí　běnzî　zài　zhuōzîshâng.
　　The exercise notebook is on the table.

14. 我的　同屋　在　学校里.
Wǒdě   tóngwū   zài   xuéxiàolǐ.
My roommate is in the school.

In such cases, we may use the word 边兒 as well. But the other nouns of locality should not be shortened in this way, for their meanings will be different when 边兒 is omitted.

We have mentioned above that the particle 的 in such a word combination as 我們前边兒 may be omitted; but when 里边兒 and 上边兒 are already shortened into monosyllabic words 里 and 上, the particle 的 should not be used. That is to say: 桌子上 and 学校里 are correct, but not 桌子的上 and 学校的里.

23.3 The Noun of Locality 里边兒   The noun of locality 里边兒 is rather peculiar in use. Some nouns require it, some don't, and still some others may or may not require it at all. The general rules are as follows:

(1) After geographical terms, we do not use 里边兒. e. g.

15. 我們　在　中国.
Wǒměn   zài   Zhōngguó.
We are in China.

16. 他的　朋友　在　北京　学習.
Tādě   péngyǒu   zài   Běijīng   xuéxí.
His friends study in Peking.

We must remember that in such cases, we never say 中国里边兒 or 北京里边兒.

(2) When the word 在 is followed by nouns such as names of buildings, organizations and so on, and if the meaning of 里边兒 is understood, then 里边兒 may or may not be omitted. e. g.

17. 他們　都　在　工厂　(里边兒)　工作.
Tāměn   dōu   zài gōngchǎng   (lǐbiǎnr)   gōngzuò.
They all work in the factory.

If the persons are not inside the factory, we must use other nouns of locality, such as 外边兒 and 旁边兒 to indicate that they are outside or by the side of the factory etc. When there is no noun of locality following the object of 在, 里边兒 is understood as a rule.

(3) Some nouns, such as the nouns denoting implements, must take nouns of locality, because there are many sides of a thing and it is difficult to ascertain where without a noun of locality. Therefore 里边兒 cannot be omitted. e. g.

18. 那　　半張　　紙　　在　　書　　里(边兒).
　　 Nèi　bànzhāng　zhǐ　zài　shū　lǐ(biānr).

That half sheet of paper is inside the book.

We cannot omit the other nouns of locality.

課文　Kèwén　Text

SIDE FIVE, BAND SEVEN

I

1. 椅子　　在　　桌子　　后边兒.
　 Yǐzi　　zài　　zhuōzi　hòubiānr.

The chair is in back of the table.

2. 桌子　　在　　椅子　　前边兒.
　 Zhuōzi　zài　　yǐzi　　qiánbiānr.

The table is in front of the chair.

3. 人民　　画报　　在　　杂誌　　下边兒.
　 Rénmín　Huàbào　zài　zázhì　xiàbiānr.

"The People's Picture Magazine" is under the magazine.

4. 杂誌　　在　　画报　　上边兒.
　 Zázhì　zài　　huàbào　shàngbiānr.

The magazine is on top of the picture news magazine.

5. 我　　同屋　　在　　宿舍(里)　唱　　歌兒.
　 Wǒ　tóngwū　zài　sùshè(lǐ)　chàng　gēr.

My roommate is singing in the dormitory.

6. 他　朋友　在　書上　写　名字.
   Tā péngyǒu zài shūshàng xiě míngzì.
   His friend writes his name on the book.

7. 我　在　本子里　作　練習.
   Wǒ zài běnzǐlǐ zuò liànxí.
   I am doing exercises in my notebook.

8. 他　在　紙上　練習　汉字.
   Tā zài zhǐshàng liànxí hànzì.
   He is practicing Chinese characters on paper.

II

(a₁)　你們的　宿舍　在　哪兒?
　　　Nǐmêndê sùshè zài nǎr?
　　　Where is your dormitory?

(b₁)　在　北京　大学　里边兒.
　　　Zài Běijīng Dàxué lǐbiânr.
　　　In Peking University.

(a₂)　你　在　什么　地方　学習?
　　　Nǐ zài shénmô dìfâng xuéxí?
　　　常常　在　宿舍(里)　学習　嗎?
　　　Chángcháng zài sùshè(lǐ) xuéxí mâ?
　　　Where (at what place) do you study? Do you study
　　　often in the dormitory?

(b₂)　我　在　圖書館(里)　学習.
　　　Wǒ zài túshūguǎn(lǐ) xuéxí.
　　　我　同屋　在　宿舍(里)　学習.
　　　Wǒ tóngwū zài sùshè(lǐ) xuéxí.
　　　I study in the library. My roommate studies in the
　　　dormitory.

III

(a₃) 你們　圖書館　在　什么　地方?
Nǐmen　túshūguǎn　zài　shénmǒ　dìfāng?
Where is your library?

(b₃) 在　礼堂　旁边兒.
Zài　lǐtáng　pángbiānr.
Beside the auditorium.

(a₄) 你　在　圖書館(里)　都　作　什么?
Nǐ　zài　túshūguǎn(lǐ)　dōu　zuò　shénmǒ?
What do you do in the library?

(b₄) 念　書,　作　練習.　我　也　看　报.
Niàn　shū,　zuò　liànxí.　Wǒ　yě　kàn　bào.

圖書館的　报　很　多.
Túshūguǎndě　bào　hěn　duō.

I study and practice. I also read newspapers. There
are many papers in the library.

(a₅) 这本　杂誌　也　是　圖書館的　吗?
Zhèiběn　zázhì　yě　shì　túshūguǎndě　mǎ?
Does this magazine belong to the library too?

(b₅) 不　是.　是　我的.　你　看,　这　是
Bú　shì.　Shì　wǒdě.　Nǐ　kàn,　zhèi　shì

我的　名字.
wǒdě　míngzi.

No. It's mine. Look, this is my name.

課外練習　Kèwài liànxí　Home Work

1) Make sentences with each of the following word
combinations:

(1) 什么　地方

(2) 在...旁边兒

2) Translate the following into Chinese:

(3) The teachers' dormitories are outside the school, the students' dormitories are inside the school.

(4) The chairs in the front of the auditorium are new ones and those at the back are old ones.

3) Complete the following sentences according to the grammar rules given in this lesson:

(5) 学生　都　在　圖書館　___.

(6) 我　同屋　在　張　同志　___.

(7) 杂誌　在　書　上边兒,　画报　在　書　下边兒,　書　在　杂誌　和　画报　___.

汉字表　Hànzì biǎo　Chinese Characters

1	在	一　ナ　大　在
2	边	
3	外	
4	上	丨　卜　上
5	下	一　丁　下
6	閒	門
		日
7	前	丷（丶　丷　丷）
		月
		刂
8	厂	一　厂

9	后	⼃ ⼚ ⼫ 后		
10	宿	宀		
		佰	亻	
			百（一百）	
11	舍	人 今 全 舍		
12	方			
13	圖	冂 冂 冋 冊 冊 周 周 圖 圖		
14	館	食		
		官（宀 宀 宀 官 官 官）		
15	礼	礻		
		⻄		
16	堂	尚		
		土		
17	旁	丶 一 二 亠 立 旁		

Lesson 24

語法復習　Yǔfǎ fùxí　Review

24.1 The Adverbial Modifier and the Complement of Degree

We know that an adjective may be used as an adverbial modifier before a verb or an adjective (20.1). It may also be used as a complement of degree after a verb or an adjective (21.2). As an adverbial modifier, the adjective is sometimes followed by the structural particle 地 and sometimes not; but as a complement of degree, it must be preceded by the structural particle 得. Whether as an adverbial modifier or as a complement or degree, the adjective always says something about the central word. Hence it is necessary here to get a clear idea of their different uses:

(1) It is very common to use an adjective as the complement of degree to a verb. In a sentence containing a complement of degree, the verb generally denotes a completed action or an action that happens frequently. e. g.

1. 他　来得　很　早.
   Tā　　láide　hěn　zǎo.
   He (generally) comes early.

2. 他　学　中文　学得　很　快.
   Tā　xué zhōngwén　xuéde　hěn　kuài.
   He learns Chinese very quickly.

Here 来 and 学 are two completed actions or actions that have continued for some time, meaning "he comes early" or "he is quick in learning". Here what we wish to express is not "whether he has come or not" or "whether he is studying or not"; because in such sentences, the actions of 来 and 学 have already happened. Now what we wish to make clear is only "how" have the actions proceeded. Therefore, a verbal sentence with a complement of degree possesses the nature of a descriptive sentence. And a sentence with an adjectival predicate followed by a complement of degree is of course a pure descriptive sentence.

(2) It is also common to use an adjective as adverbial modifier of a verb. In a sentence containing such an adverbial modifier, the action is not restricted by time, because in this kind of sentence the adverbial modifier is used to describe the way or manner of the action, and not to describe the extent or result of the action. Therefore, this kind of sentence with a verbal predicate is more narrative in nature.

24.2 The Use of the Structural Particle 地 after the Adverbial Modifier The adverbial modifier is sometimes followed by the structural particle 地, and sometimes not. The following rules show when this particle 地 is needed:

(1) 地 should never be used under the following conditions:

a) If the adverbial modifier is a monosyllabic word (it may be an adverb or an adjective), the particle 地 is not used. e.g.

3. 他 不 去.
  Tā bú qù.
  He is not going.

4. 我 一定 早 来.
  Wǒ yídìng zǎo lái.
  I will surely come early.

b) If the adverbial modifier is a prepositional construction, the particle 地 is not used. e. g.

5. 他們 从 礼堂 来.
  Tāmén cóng lǐtáng lái.
  They are coming from the auditorium.

6. 我 跟 張 同志 跳 舞.
  Wǒ gēn Zhāng tóngzhì tiào wǔ.
  I dance with Comrade Chāng.

(2) 地 is often not used. If the adverbial modifier is a dissyllabic adverb, 地 is generally not used. e. g.

7. 我們　一起　學習.
Wǒmén　yìqǐ　xuéxí.
We study together.

There are a few dissyllabic adverbs that can be followed by the particle, but it is more idiomatic not to use it. e. g.

8. 他　常常(地)　唱　歌兒.
Tā　chángcháng(dě) chàng　gēr.
He sings frequently. (OR: He often sings.)

(3) 地 is often used.　If the adverbial modifier is made up of a dissyllabic adjective or a reduplicated adjective, the particle 地 is more often used than not. e. g.

9. 他們　都　积極地　工作.
Tāmén　dōu　jījídě　gōngzuò.
They all work enthusiastically.

10. 我　一定　好好兒地　學習　中文.
Wǒ　yídìng　hǎohāordě　xuéxí　zhōngwén.
I will surely study Chinese well.

11. 朋友　都　高高兴兴地　唱　歌兒.
Péngyǒu dōu　gāogǎoxìngxìngdě chàng　gēr.
All the friends sing very gladly.

(4) 地 must be used.　In general, when an adjective used as an adverbial modifier is modified by another adverbial modifier, the particle must be used. e. g.

12. 他　很　努力地　學習.
Tā　hěn　nǔlìdě　xuéxí.
He studies very diligently.

課文 Kèwén Text

SIDE SIX, BAND ONE

I

(a₁) 你 从 哪兒 来?
Nǐ cóng nǎr lái?

Where are you coming from?

(b₁) 我 从 圖書館 来.
Wǒ cóng túshūguǎn lái.

I'm coming from the library.

(a₂) 你 在 圖書館 作 什么?
Nǐ zài túshūguǎn zuò shénmǒ?

What do you do in the library?

(b₂) 学習 中文, 我 在 那兒 看 書,
Xuéxí zhōngwén, wǒ zài nàr kàn shū,

写 汉字, 作 練習.
xiě hànzì, zuò liànxí.

I study Chinese; there I read, write characters and do
my exercises.

(a₃) 你 不 看 电影 嗎?
Nǐ bú kàn diànyǐng mǎ?

Won't you see the film?

(b₃) 什么 电影? 是 苏联 电影 嗎?
Shénmǒ diànyǐng? Shì Sūlián diànyǐng mǎ?

What film? Is it a Soviet film?

(a₄) 不 是, 是 中国的. 你 喜欢 不 喜
Bú shì, shì Zhōngguóde. Nǐ xǐhuān bù xǐ-

欢 中国 电影?
huān Zhōngguó diànyǐng?

No, it's Chinese. Do you like Chinese films?

(b₄) 喜欢, 很 多 中国 电影 都 很
Xǐhuān, hěn duō Zhōngguó diànyǐng dōu hěn

好, 都 很 有意思.
hǎo, dōu hěn yǒuyìsi.

I do, many Chinese films are (very) good and (very) interesting.

II

(a₅) 張 先生 在 哪兒?
Zhāng xiānshěng zài nǎr?

Where is Mr. Chāng?

(b₅) 他 在 学生 宿舍(里).
Tā zài xuéshěng sùshè(li).

He is in the students' dormitory.

(a₆) 他 在 学生 宿舍(里) 作 什么?
Tā zài xuéshěng sùshè(li) zuò shénmǒ?

What is he doing in the students' dormitory?

(b₆) 他 在 那兒 跟 学生 説 話.
Tā zài nàr gēn xuéshěng shuō huà.

He is speaking with the students there.

(a₇) 他們 説 哪国 話?
Tāmén shuō něiguó huà?

What language do they speak?

(b₇) 説 中国 話. 張 先生 是 中文
Shuō Zhōngguó huà. Zhāng xiānshēng shì zhōngwén

先生. 他 跟 学生 只 説 中文.
xiānshēng. Tā gēn xuéshēng zhǐ shuō zhōngwén.

Chinese. Mr. Chāng teaches Chinese. He speaks only
Chinese with the students.

(a₈) 学生 都 懂 嗎?
Xuéshēng dōu dǒng má?

Do the students understand?

(b₈) 張 先生 説 中文, 学生 都 懂.
Zhāng xiānshēng shuō zhōngwén, xuéshēng dōu dǒng.

他 説 中文 説得 很 慢, 他
Tā shuō zhōngwén shuōdě hěn màn. Tā

常常 跟 学生 説 話, 学生 都
chángcháng gēn xuéshēng shuō huà, xuéshēng dōu

懂 他的 話.
dǒng tādě huà.

Mr. Chāng speaks Chinese; the students all understand. He speaks Chinese very slowly. He often
speaks with the students, and the students understand
what he says.

Lesson 25

生詞 Shēngcí New Words
SIDE SIX, BAND TWO

1.	月	(名) yuè	month
2.	今天	(名) jīntiān	today
3.	日	(名) rì	day
4.	号	(名) hào	day, number
5.	星期	(名) xīngqī	week
6.	天	(名) tiān	day
7.	点(鐘)	(名) diǎn(zhōng)	o'clock
8.	过	(动) guò	to pass, past
9.	分	(名) fēn	minute
10.	刻	(名) kè	a quarter
11.	差	(动) chà	less
12.	忙	(形) máng	busy
13.	今年	(名) jīnnián	this year
14.	现在	(名) xiànzài	now, at present
15.	时候兒	(名) shíhòur	time

語法 Yǔfǎ Grammar

25.1 **Nouns of Time** In Chinese, some nouns are exclusively used to indicate time. So far as their functions are concerned, they are just the same as other nouns. They may all be used as subject, object, adjective modifier etc. in a sentence.

1. 一年　有　十二个　月.
Yìnián　yǒu　shíèrge　yuè.

There are twelve months in a year. (LIT.: One year has twelve months.)

2. 这　是　今天的　报.
Zhèi　shì　jīntiānde　bào.

This is today's paper.

一年 is subject, 十二个月 is object, and 今天 is the adjective modifier of 报.

25.2 **The Expressions of Year, Month, Day and Hour** In Chinese, indication of time begins from the biggest unit to the smallest unit, that is to say: 年 stands first, 月 second, 日 third, and then 时.

The year is always expressed in a simple way, e.g. "1957" is always read as 一九五七年, only very occasionally read as 一千九百五十七年 (one thousand nine hundred fifty seven). In a question, we use 哪 or 几, such as 哪年 or 一九五几年.

The designation of "months" in Chinese is very simple; the names of the twelve months in a year are formed by putting the numerals 1—12 before the word 月. Such as: 一月 (January) 二月 (February)... 十月 (October), 十一月 (November) and 十二月 (December). In a question, we say 几月.

The designation of "days" is also very simple. We have only to place the numerals 1—31 before 日 or 号. 日 is formal and often used in the written language, while 号 is always used in the spoken language. e. g. 二日 (号), 十日 (号) and 三十日 (号). In asking questions, we use 几号, 十几号, 二十几号.

In naming the seven days of the week, we place the numerals 1—6 after the word 星期. For example: 星期一 (Monday), 星期二 (Tuesday)... 星期五 (Friday) and 星期六 (Saturday); the seventh day in a week is called 星期日 (Sunday), it can also be shortened as 星期. In a question, we say 星期几.

Note: We can only say 一个月有三十天 (or 三十一天) and 一个星期有七天, but we cannot say 一个月有三十号 (or 三十一号), and 一个星期有七号.

Time of the day is shown in the following:

3. 12:00 十二点（钟）
shíèrdiǎn (zhōng)

4. 12:05 十二点 （过） 五分
shíèrdiǎn (guò) wǔfēn
(LIT.: twelve o'clock [past] five minutes)

5. 12:15 十二点 十五分
shíèrdiǎn shíwǔfēn

十二点 一刻
shíèrdiǎn yíkè
(LIT.: twelve o'clock one quarter)

6. 12:30 十二点 半（钟）
shíèrdiǎn bàn(zhōng)
(LIT.: twelve o'clock half)

十二点 三十分
shíèrdiǎn sānshífēn

7. 12:45 十二点 三刻
shíèrdiǎn sānkè
(LIT.: twelve o'clock three quarters)

十二点 四十五分
shíèrdiǎn sìshíwǔfēn

差 一刻 一点
chà yíkè yìdiǎn
(LIT.: less one quarter one o'clock)

8. 12:55 十二点 五十五分
shíèrdiǎn wǔshíwǔfēn

差 五分 一点
chà wǔfēn yìdiǎn
(LIT.: less five minutes one o'clock)

Therefore in a date, when the year, the month, the day and the hour are given at the same time, the word order is as follows:

9.　一九五七年　十月　一日（星期二）　十点
　　yījiǔwǔqīnián　shíyuè　yírì　(xīngqīèr)　shídiǎn
ten o'clock, (Tuesday), October 1, 1957 (LIT.: one-nine-five-seven-year ten-month one-day [week-two] ten-o'clock)

25.3 Words and Word Groups of Time Used as Adverbial Modifiers Words of time are not only used as subjects, objects and adjective modifiers, but also frequently as adverbial modifiers. When we wish to tell the time or period of a certain action, we use a word or word group of time as adverbial modifier. e. g.

10.　我　七点半　去.
　　Wǒ　qīdiǎnbàn　qù.
I am going at 7:30.

11.　他　星期二　很　忙.
　　Tā　xīngqīèr　hěn　máng.
He is very busy on Tuesdays.

七点半 and 星期二 are both words of time. The adverbial modifier, 七点半, gives the time of 去, and 星期二 tells when he is busy. More examples are:

12.　我們　一天　学　十八个　汉字.
　　Wǒmen　yìtiān　xué　shíbágè　hànzì.
We learn eighteen Chinese characters in one day.

13.　我的　朋友　这个　月　很　忙.
　　Wǒdě　péngyǒu　zhèigě　yuè　hěn　máng.
My friend is very busy this month.

一天 and 这个月 both represent certain periods of time. Here 天 indicates the time of the action 学汉字, and 这个月 tells when the state of 忙 (being busy) takes place.

When we wish to emphasize time, we may put the word or word group of time at the beginning of a sentence. e. g.

14. 星期二　他　很　忙.
　　Xīngqīèr　tā　hěn　máng.
　　On Tuesdays he is very busy.

15. 一天　我們　学　十八个　汉字.
　　Yìtiān　wǒmen　xué　shíbágè　hànzì.
　　In one day we learn eighteen Chinese characters.

25.4 有　有 is a verb, but it does not express any action. It shows a relation of ownership, and its subject is always a noun or pronoun denoting a person or persons. But if we wish to tell how many persons or things there are in a certain place, or how many smaller units there are in a definite period of time, we also use the verb 有. In such a case, the word or word group denoting place or time is the subject. e. g.

16. 一年　有　十二个　月.
　　Yìnián　yǒu　shíèrgè　yuè.
　　There are twelve months in a year. (LIT.: One year has twelve months.)

17. 北京　大学　有　很　多　学生.
　　Běijīng　Dàxué　yǒu　hěn　duō　xuéshēng.
　　There are many students in Peking University.

18. 圖書館里　有　很　多　書.
　　Túshūguǎnlǐ　yǒu　hěn　duō　shū.
　　There are many books in the library.

The above-mentioned sentences are by structure similar to the sentences 我有書 and 你有报. 一年, 北京大学 and 圖書館里 are subjects. Therefore, it is idiomatic, especially in the spoken language, not to use the preposition 在 before the word or word group expressing place or time. We never say 在一年有十二个月 or 在北京大学有很多学生.

課文   Kèwén   Text

SIDE SIX, BAND TWO

(a₁)   今年　是　一九六几年？
　　　Jīnnián　shì　yījiǔliùjǐnián?

What year is this (of the 1960's)?

(b₁)   今年　是　一九六一年.
　　　Jīnnián　shì　yījiǔliùyīnián.

This is 1961.

(a₂)   这个　月　是　几月？
　　　Zhèige　yuè　shì　jǐyuè?

What month is this?

(b₂)   这个　月　是　三月.
　　　Zhèige　yuè　shì　sānyuè.

This is March.

(a₃)   今天　是　几月　几号？
　　　Jīntiān　shì　jǐyuè　jǐhào?

What is the month and date today?

(b₃)   今天　是　三月　二十二号.
　　　Jīntiān　shì　sānyuè　èrshíèrhào.

Today is March twenty-second.

(a₄)   今天　是　星期几？
　　　Jīntiān　shì　xīngqījǐ?

What day of the week is today?

(b₄) 今天　是　星期三.
Jīntiān shì xīngqīsān.

Today is Wednesday.

(a₅) 一个　星期　有　几天?
Yígė xīngqī yǒu jǐtiān?

How many days are there in a week?

(b₅) 一个　星期　有　七天.
Yígė xīngqī yǒu qītiān.

There are seven days in a week.

(a₆) 这　七天的　名字　都　叫　什么?
Zhèi qītiāndė míngzı dōu jiào shénmȯ?

What are the names of these seven days?

(b₆) 这　七天　叫:　星期一、星期二、星
Zhèi qītiān jiào: xīngqīyī、 xīngqièr、 xīng-

期三、星期四、星期五、星期六、
qīsān、 xīngqīsì、 xīngqīwǔ、 xīngqīliù、

星期日.
xīngqīrì.

These seven days are called Monday, Tuesday, Wednesday, Thursday, Friday, Saturday and Sunday.

(a₇) 现在　是　几点　几分?
Xiànzài shì jǐdiǎn jǐfēn?

What time is it? (LIT.: Now is how many hours how many minutes?)

(b₇) 现在　是　两点　过　一刻.
Xiànzài shì liǎngdiǎn guò yíkè.

It's a quarter after two. (LIT.: Now is two o'clock past a quarter.)

(a₈) 先生 什么 时候兒 来?
Xiānshēng shénmō shíhôur lái?

At what time is the teacher coming?

(b₈) 先生 两点半 来.
Xiānshēng liǎngdiǎnbàn lái.

The teacher is coming at two-thirty.

(a₉) 这个 星期六 你 看 电影 吗?
Zhèigê xīngqīliù nǐ kàn diànyǐng mâ?

Are you seeing a film this Saturday?

(b₉) 看, 这个 星期六 我 看 电影.
Kàn, zhèigê xīngqīliù wǒ kàn diànyǐng.

Yes, this Saturday I'm seeing a film.

課外練習 Kèwài liànxí Home Work

1) Put the following units of time into Chinese:

    (1) 7:05 (2) 4:50 (3) 8:30 (4) 11:00

    (5) May first (1st of May) — Wednesday

    (6) 8th of March 1958

2) Write out appropriate questions for the following sentences:

    (7) 今天 是 星期五.

    (8) 现在 是 十二点 过 十分.

    (9) 一个 星期 有 七天.

    (10) 我的 朋友 四月 三号 来.

3) Answer the following questions:

(11) 你 星期日 学习 不 学习?

(12) 这个 星期 你 哪天 忙, 哪天 不 忙?

汉字表   Hànzì biǎo Chinese Characters

1	月	
2	今	
3	天	一 天
4	日	
5	号	口 口 号
6	星	日
		生
7	期	其 (一 十 廿 冊 甘 丗 其)
		月
8	点	占
		灬
9	鐘	金
		童	立
			里
10	过	寸
		辶

11	分	
12	刻	亥 (、 二 亥 亥 亥 亥)
		刂
13	差	、 ⍀ ⸚ 丷 羊 羊 羊 差
14	忙	忄
		亡 (、 二 亡)
15	現	王 (⁻ 二 干 王)
	見	目
		儿
16	时	日
		寸
17	候	亻 亻 仆 仁 候

Lesson 26

生詞 Shēngcí New Words

SIDE SIX, BAND THREE

1. 能	(能动) néng	to be able, can
2. 会	(能动) huì	can, may
3. 要	(动、能动) yào	to want, should
4. 应該	(能动) yīnggāi	should, ought
5. 用	(动) yòng	to use
6. 字典	(名) zìdiǎn	dictionary
7. 認識	(动、名) rènshi	to know, to recognize
8. 还	(副) hái	also, too, still
9. 以后	(副) yǐhòu	afterwards
10. 买	(动) mǎi	to buy
11. 听	(动) tīng	to hear, to listen to
12. 好看	(形) hǎokàn	good-looking
13. 沒关系	méiguānxi	never mind, it does n't matter
14. 觉得	(动) juéde	to feel
15. 东西	(名) dōngxi	thing

語法 Yǔfǎ Grammar

26.1 **Optative Verbs (verbs of ability and willingness)**
Optative verbs belong to the part of speech of verbs. But they are different from other common verbs, because they have their own grammatical characteristics: they are never used redu-

plicatively and never followed by any suffix or any substantive
object; they are used before verbs or adjectives. The main
function of optative verbs is to indicate possibility, ability,
willingness, demand or intention.

(1) 能　能 implies subjective ability. e. g.

1. 他　一天　能　看　一本　中文　書.
   Tā　yìtiān　néng　kàn　yìběn　zhōngwén　shū.

   He can read a Chinese book in one day.

2. 我　十分鐘　能　寫　很　多　汉字.
   Wǒ　shífēnzhōng　néng　xiě　hěn　duō　hànzì.

   I can write many Chinese characters in fifteen minutes
   (time).

Sometimes it implies permission under certain conditions. e.g.

3. 我們　不　能　在　圖書館里　說　話.
   Wǒmen　bù　néng　zài　túshūguǎnlǐ　shuō　huà.

   We cannot talk in the library.

4. 我　能　跟　你　一起　作　練習　嗎?
   Wǒ　néng　gēn　nǐ　yìqǐ　zuò　liànxí　má?

   Can I (or: May I) do the exercise (together) with
   you?

(2) 会　会 is a verb, but it is also an optative verb used
before a verb or an adjective. When it is used as an optative
verb, it also implies subjective ability, but it is different from
能, because 会 means a certain skill acquired through learning,
so it is often similar to 精通 (to be well-versed) and 掌握 (to
master) in meaning. e. g.

5. 他　会　說　中文.
   Tā　huì　shuō　zhōngwén.

   He can (or: knows how to) speak Chinese.

6. 这个　同志　会　跳　舞.
   Zhèigè　tóngzhì　huì　tiào　wǔ.

   This comrade can dance.

說中文 and 跳舞 in the above examples are skills acquired through learning.

会 sometimes implies a possibility under certain conditions. e. g.

7. 这本　杂誌　不　会　是　他的.
Zhèiběn　zázhì　bú　huì　shì　tādě.

This magazine can't be his.

8. 他　在　礼堂　看　电影, 不　会　在
Tā　zài　lǐtáng　kàn　diànyǐng,　bú　huì　zài

圖書館.
túshūguǎn.

He is seeing a film in the auditorium, he can't be in the library.

(3) 要　Like the word 会, 要 is a verb. e. g.

9. 先生　要　一張　干淨　紙.
Xiānshěng　yào　yìzhāng　gānjǐng　zhǐ.

The teacher wants a clean sheet of paper.

When 要 is used as an optative verb, it indicates subjective desire or intention. e. g.

10. 我　要　去　圖書館.
Wǒ　yào　qù　túshūguǎn.

I want to go to the library.

11. 先生　要　看　你的　本子.
Xiānshěng　yào　kàn　nǐdě　běnzǐ.

The teacher wants to look at your notebook.

It sometimes indicates objective necessity.

12. 学生　要　好好兒地　学習.
Xuéshěng　yào　hǎohāordě　xuéxí.

A student must study very well.

13. 黑板　要　干淨.
Hēibǎn　yào　gānjìng.

The blackboard must be clean.

Note: 要 in example 13 is used before an adjective.

(4) 应該　应該 expresses some demand or necessity dictated by reason or habit. That is to say, it is not right or proper not to do so. e. g.

14. 我們　应該　看　这本　杂誌.
Wǒmén　yīnggāi　kàn　zhèiběn　zázhì.

We ought to read this magazine.

15. 学生　都　应該　努力.
Xuéshēng　dōu　yīnggāi　nǔlì.

All students ought to be diligent.

Note: The optative verb 应該 may be followed by an adjective.

26.2 Some Rules Concerning Optative Verbs
(1) If an optative verb is used in the alternative interrogative sentence, we need only give both the affirmative and the negative forms of the optative verb. e. g.

16. 你　能　不　能　来?
Nǐ　néng　bù　néng　lái?

Can you come (or not)?

17. 你　要　不　要　跟　我　一起　去?
Nǐ　yào　bú　yào　gēn　wǒ　yìqǐ　qù?

Do you want to go (together) with me?

If the predicate is simple and short, the element after the optative verb may be used two times. e. g.

18. 你　能　来　不　能　(来)?
Nǐ　néng　lái　bù　néng　(lái)?

Can you come?

Note: In such interrogative sentences, the optative verb has to be repeated. So we cannot say 能来不来. But the second form of the verb may be omitted.

(2) In answering questions, the optative verb may stand alone and be used as the predicate. e. g.

19. 你　要　看　报　吗?
    Nǐ　yào　kàn　bào　mǎ?
    Do you want to read the newspaper?

20. 要.
    Yào.
    Yes (I want to).

21. 你　会　不　会　用　中文　字典?
    Nǐ　huì　bú　huì　yòng　zhōngwén　zìdiǎn?
    Do you know how to use a Chinese dictionary?

22. 会.
    Huì.
    Yes.

(3) Two optative verbs may be used in succession. e. g.

23. 学生　应該　会　念　这些　汉字.
    Xuéshēng　yīnggāi　huì　niàn　zhèixiē　hànzì.
    Students ought to be able to read these characters.

24. 他　今天　沒　有　工作,　应該　能
    Tā　jīntiān　méi　yǒu　gōngzuò,　yīnggāi　néng
    来.
    lái.
    He has no work to do today, he should be able to come.

課文 Kèwén Text

SIDE SIX, BAND THREE

(a₁) 現在 你們 能 看 中文 报 嗎?
Xiànzài nǐmen néng kàn zhōngwén bào mǎ?

Can you read a Chinese newspaper now?

(b₁) 不 能, 我們 只 認識 很 少的
Bù néng, wǒmen zhǐ rènshi hěn shǎode

汉字, 还 不 能 看 报.
hànzì, hái bù néng kàn bào.

No, we recognize only a few characters, and we still can't read a newspaper.

(a₂) 你們 会 用 字典 不 会?
Nǐmen huì yòng zìdiǎn bú huì?

Do you know how to use a dictionary?

(b₂) 現在 还 不 会, 以后 先生 要
Xiànzài hái bú huì, yǐhòu xiānshēng yào

教 我們. 我們 应該 会 用 字典.
jiāo wǒmen. Wǒmen yīnggāi huì yòng zìdiǎn.

We still don't know (how); later the teacher intends to teach us (how). We ought to know how to use a dictionary.

(a₃) 你 有 沒 有 字典?
Nǐ yǒu méi yǒu zìdiǎn?

Do you have a dictionary?

(b₃) 沒 有, 我 一定 要 买 一本.
Méi yǒu, wǒ yídìng yào mǎi yìběn.

我 学習 中文, 应該 有 字典.
Wǒ xuéxí zhōngwén, yīnggāi yǒu zìdiǎn.

No, (but) I surely intend to buy one. I study Chinese, and I ought to have a dictionary.

(a₄) 你們　学習　中文,　只　要　会　説
Nǐmen　xuéxí　zhōngwén,　zhǐ　yào　huì　shuō

話、会　看　書　嗎?
huà、huì　kàn　shū　må?

You are studying Chinese; do you want to be able to
speak and read only?

(b₄) 不,　我們　应該　能　听、能　説、能
Bù,　wǒmen　yīnggāi　néng　tīng、néng　shuō、néng

念、能　写.
niàn、néng　xiě.

No, we ought to be able to understand (Chinese when
spoken), to speak it, to read it.and to write it.

(a₅) 你們　也　会　写　汉字　嗎?
Nǐmen　yě　huì　xiě　hànzì　må?

Do you know how to write Chinese characters also?

(b₅) 对　了,　我們　会　写　一些.　我們
Duì　le,　wǒmen　huì　xiě　yìxiē.　Wǒmen

写得　慢,　写得　不　好看.
xiědė　màn,　xiědė　bù　hǎokàn.

Right, we know how to write a few. We write slowly,
and don't write them well (LIT.: write not good-
looking).

(a₆) 沒　关系,　你們　常常　練習,　一定
Méi　guānxì,　nǐmen　chángcháng　liànxí,　yídìng

能　写得　很　好.　你們　觉得
néng　xiědė　hěn　hǎo.　Nǐmen　juédė

怎么样?　很　忙　嗎?
zěnmốyàng?　Hěn　máng　må?

No matter, practice often and you will certainly be
able to write them well. How do you feel? Very busy?

(b₆) 我們　很　忙．　我們　一年　要
　　　Wǒmen　hěn　máng.　Wǒmen　yìnián　yào

学習　很　多　东西，我們　应該
xuéxí　hěn　duō　dōngxi,　wǒmen　yīnggāi

忙.
máng.

We are very busy. We want to learn many things in one year, and we should be busy.

課外練習　Kèwài liànxí　Home Work

1) Write questions with each of the following words, and after that answer them:

(1) 能　　　　(2) 会

(3) 要　　　　(4) 应該

2) Transcribe the following Chinese characters, and compare the different pronunciation of each group:

(5) 以　意

(6) 看　干

(7) 知　只　枝　誌　纸　志

汉字表　Hànzì biǎo　Chinese Characters

l	能	ム
		月
		ヒ（し ヒ）
		ヒ

2	要	西		
		女		
3	应	广 广 广 应 应		
4	該	言		
		亥		
5	用	丿 冂 月 月 用		
6	典	丶 冂 日 由 曲 曲 典		
7	認	言		
		忍	刃 (刀 刃)	
			心	
8	識	言		
		戠	音	立
				日
			戈	
9	还	不		
		辶		
10	以	𠃊 𠃊 以 以		
11	买	乛 乛 乛 买 买 买		
12	听	口		
		斤		
13	关			

14	系	ノ ㄠ ㄠ 玄 系
15	觉	⺍
		见
16	东	一 セ 车 东 东
17	西	

Lesson 27

生詞 Shēngcí New Words

1.	上(星期)	(形)	shàng (xīngqī)	last (week)
2.	下(星期)	(形)	xià (xīngqī)	next (week)
3.	了	(尾、助)	lē	(a suffix and a particle)
4.	从前	(副)	cóngqián	in the past, formerly
5.	明天	(名)	míngtiān	tomorrow
6.	昨天	(名)	zuótiān	yesterday
7.	回	(动)	huí	to go back, to return
8.	句子	(名)	jùzĭ	sentence
9.	就	(副)	jiù	then, at once,
10.	呢	(助)	nē	(a particle)
11.	講	(动)	jiǎng	to explain, to give a lecture on, to tell
12.	清楚	(形)	qīngchǔ	clear
13.	复习	(动)	fùxí	to review
14.	词彙	(名)	cíhuì	vocabulary
15.	语法	(名)	yǔfǎ	grammar
16.	进	(动)	jìn	to enter
17.	城	(名)	chéng	city, town

語法 Yǔfǎ Grammar

27.1 **The Perfective Aspect** In Chinese, the time of an action, whether it is of the past, present or future, is expressed mainly by a word or word group of time. e. g.

1. 我們　上星期六　看　电影，　你們
   Wǒmēn　shàngxīngqīliù　kàn　diànyǐng,　nǐmēn

   下星期六　看　电影.
   xiàxīngqīliù　kàn　diànyǐng.

   We saw a film last Saturday, you (plural) will see a film next Saturday.

The time of action is indicated by the adverbial modifiers of time 上星期六 and 下星期六. The verb 看 has nothing in its morphology to express the time.

But in Chinese, the aspect of an action is very important. An action may be in its starting, progressive, continuous or completed state, and a verb may have various kinds of aspects accordingly. In today's lesson, we will discuss only the perfective aspect. In Chinese, aspects are shown by suffixes and the suffix 了 is used to indicate the aspect of a completed action. When we wish to stress the completion of an action, we use the suffix 了 after the verb. e. g.

2. 他　来　了.
   Tā　lái　lé.

   He has come. (or: He came.)

3. 我們　懂　了.
   Wǒmēn　dǒng　lé.

   We understand (=We have understood).

There are two points to be noticed with regard to the perfective aspect:

(1) The suffix 了 does not indicate past time. Even if the time of an action is in the past, we do not use the suffix 了, unless we want to emphasize the completion of the action. e. g.

4. 他　一九五四年　在　这兒　工作.
Tā　　yǐjiǔwǔsìnián　zài　zhèr　gōngzuò.
He worked here in 1954.

5. 从前　他　常常　来.
Cóngqián　tā　chángcháng　lái.
In the past he came frequently. (OR: He used to come often before.)

(2) The suffix 了 may also be used to stress the completion of an action in the future. e. g.

6. 明天　你們　来了,　我們　一起　跳　舞.
Míngtiān　nǐmen　láile,　wǒmen　yìqǐ　tiào　wǔ.
When you (plural) come tomorrow, we will dance together. (LIT.: Tomorrow you come-COMPLETION, we together dance.)

This kind of perfective aspect is generally used to show the order of actions in a sentence, for the second action only happens after the completion of the first one.

27.2　了 and the Object　When we use the suffix 了 in a sentence in which there is an object, the following three points have to be observed:

(1)　了 is generally used after the verb and before the object, especially when the object is modified by an adjective modifier. e. g.

7. 我　昨天　买了　一本　画报.
Wǒ　zuótiān　mǎile　yìběn　huàbào.
Yesterday I bought a picture news magazine.

8. 星期日　我　看了　那本　杂誌.
Xīngqīrì　wǒ　kànle　nèiběn　zázhì.
I read that magazine on Sunday.

(2) In a simple sentence, the suffix 了 is used after the verb, and the modal particle 了 is used after the object. e. g.

9. 昨天　我　作(了)　練習　了.
Zuótiān　wǒ　zuò(le)　liànxí　le.

I did the exercises yesterday.

10. 他　回(了)　宿舍　了.
Tā　huí(le)　sùshè　le.

He has returned to the dormitory.

In such sentences, the suffix 了 may be omitted, the particle 了 then takes on the meaning of completion. But notice the use of 了, when the object is preceded by a numeral and a measure word. When there is only the suffix 了, we mean that the action is already concluded; when both the suffix 了 and the particle 了 are used at the same time, we mean that the action is still in progression or is being continued. e. g.

11. 我　昨天　作了　八个　句子.
Wǒ　zuótiān　zuòle　bágè　jùzi.

I did eight sentences yesterday.

12. 我　作了　八个　句子　了,　现在
Wǒ　zuòle　bágè　jùzi　le,　xiànzài

要　作　下边兒的.
yào　zuò　xiàbiānrde.

I have done eight sentences (so far), now I want to do the following ones.

(3) If there is only the suffix 了 after the verb and no particle 了 after a simple object, the sentence is not complete and must be completed by adding other elements. e. g.

13. 我　作了　練習　就　去.
Wǒ　zuòle　liànxí　jiù　qù.

After I finish the exercises I will go. (LIT.: I do-COMPLETION exercises then go.)

14. 他　学了　中文　就　能　看　中文
　　Tā　xuéle　zhōngwén　jiù　néng　kàn zhōngwén

書.
shū.

After he learns Chinese he will be able to read Chinese books.

Here the adverb 就 is always used to express successive actions or the relation of cause and effect.

27.3 **The Negative Form of the Perfective Aspect**　When we wish to express an action that did not take place, we have only to add 沒有 before the verb. e. g.

15. 昨天　他　沒（有）来.
　　Zuótiān　tā　méi　yǒu　lái.

He didn't come yesterday.

16. 星期六　我　沒（有）去　圖書館.
　　Xīngqīliù　wǒ　méi　(yǒu)　qù　túshūguǎn.

I didn't go to the library on Saturday.

We have to pay attention to the fact that the affirmative suffix 了 can never be used simultaneously with 沒有, which is the negative form of the perfective aspect. Therefore, we must not say: 昨天他沒(有)来了 or 星期六我沒(有)去了圖書館.

If an action is not yet completed, and is to be completed very soon, we use the construction 还沒(有)…呢 (not yet...), the 呢 here is a modal particle. e. g.

17. 我　今天　还　沒（有）看　报　呢!
　　Wǒ　jīntiān　hái　méi　(yǒu)　kàn　bào　ne!

I have not yet read the newspaper today.

沒有 may be always shortened as 沒, whenever it is used before a verb, but when 沒有 is used independently to answer a question, it should never be shortened. e. g.

18. 先生　来　了　嗎?
　　Xiānsheng　lái　le　ma?

Has the teacher come?

19. 沒　有.
Méi　yǒu.
No (He hasn't).

20. 沒　来.
Méi　lái.
No (He hasn't come).

21. 还　沒（有）来　呢!
Hái　méi　(yǒu)　lái　ne!
Not yet (He hasn't come yet).

27.4 **The Alternative Interrogative Sentence of the Perfective
Aspect** If we wish to ask a question using the alternative
interrogative sentence, we have only to use this sentence pattern
……了 (object) 沒有. e. g.

22. 报　来　了　沒　有?
Bào　lái　le　méi　yǒu?
Has the newspaper come (or not)?

23. 你　作了　練習　沒　有?
Nǐ　zuòle　liànxí　méi　yǒu?
Have you done the exercises?

Here 沒有 cannot be shortened as 沒 either.

課文　Kèwén　Text
SIDE SIX, BAND FOUR

I

(a₁)　今天的　練習　有　八个　句子,　你
Jīntiānde　liànxí　yǒu　bágè　jùzi,　nǐ
作了　几个　了?
zuòle　jǐgè　le?
There are eight sentences in today's exercise; how
many have you done?

(b₁) 作了　四个　了.
Zuòlě sìgě lě.
I've done four.

(a₂) 你　会　作　后边兒的　那　四个　吗?
Nǐ huì zuò hòubiānrdě nèi sìgě mǎ?
Do you know how to do those four that come later?

(b₂) 先生　講得　很　清楚,　我　都　懂
Xiānshěng jiǎngdě hěn qīngchǔ, wǒ dōu dǒng
了,　我　会　作.
lě, wǒ huì zuò.
The teacher explained them very clearly and I understood everything, so I know how to do them.

(a₃) 你　复習了　从前的　詞彙　沒　有?
Nǐ fùxílě cóngqiándě cíhuì méi yǒu?
Have you reviewed the previous vocabulary words?

(b₃) 还　沒　有　复習　呢!　我　明天　复習.
Hái méi yǒu fùxí ně! Wǒ míngtiān fùxí.
Not yet. I'll review them tomorrow.

(a₄) 复習了　詞彙,　你　作　什么?
Fùxílě cíhuì, nǐ zuò shénmò?
After you review the vocabulary, what will you do?

(b₄) 复習了　詞彙,　我　就　复習　語法.
Fùxílě cíhuì, wǒ jiù fùxí yǔfǎ.
After I review the vocabulary, I will then review the grammar.

(a₅) 复習了　詞彙　和　語法,　你　还　要　作
Fùxílě cíhuì hé yǔfǎ, nǐ hái yào zuò
什么?
shénmò?
After you review the vocabulary and the grammar, what else do you intend to do?

(b₅) 复习了　词彙　和　語法,　我　就　練習
Fùxíle　cíhuì　hé　yǔfǎ,　wǒ　jiù　liànxí
汉字.
hànzì.

After I review the vocabulary and the grammar, I will then practice the characters.

II

(a₆) 上星期六　你　作　什么　了?
Shàngxīngqīliù　nǐ　zuò　shénmo　le?

What did you do last Saturday?

(b₆) 我　进　城　了.
Wǒ　jìn　chéng　le.

I went into the city.

(a₇) 你　在　城里　看了　电影　没　有?
Nǐ　zài　chénglǐ　kànle　diànyíng　méi　yǒu?

Did you see a film in the city?

(b₇) 没　有,　我　买　东西　了.
Méi　yǒu,　wǒ　mǎi　dōngxî　le.

No, I went shopping (LIT.: bought things).

(a₈) 你　买　什么　东西　了?
Nǐ　mǎi　shénmo　dōngxî　le?

What (things) did you buy?

(b₈) 我　买了　一本　字典　和　很　多　杂誌.
Wǒ　mǎile　yìběn　zìdiǎn　hé　hěn　duō　zázhì.

I bought a dictionary and a lot of magazines.

(a₉) 你　没　(有)　买　書　吗?
Nǐ　méi　(yǒu)　mǎi　shū　mǎ?

Didn't you buy books?

(b₉) 沒　有.
Méi　yǒu.

No.

課外練習　Kèwài liànxí　Home Work

1) Re-write the following sentences using Chinese characters and underline the suffix 了:
   (1) Zhèigè yuèdê "Rénmín Huàbào" lái lê.
   (2) Wǒ zuòlê liànxí jiù gēn nǐ chàng gēr.
   (3) Tā xīngqīrì méi yǒu jìn chéng, zài xuéxiào fùxí yǔfǎ lê.

2) Answer the following questions in the negative:
   (4) 你　同屋　回　宿舍　了　沒　有?
   (5) 先生　講　这些　句子　了　嗎?
   (6) 他　用了　这本　字典　沒　有?

3) Complete the following sentences:
   (7) 听了　唱　歌兒.............................
   (8) 我　进了　圖書館.............................

汉字表　Hànzì biǎo　Chinese Characters

1	明	日
		月
2	昨	日
		乍
3	回	丶 冂 冋 回
4	句	丿 勹 句
5	就	京
		尤 (一 尢 尢 尤)

6	呢		
7	講	言	
		冓（一 ＝ ≠ 냐 丼 芇 菁 冓）	
8	清	氵	
		青	
9	楚	林	木
			木
		足（一 ㄒ 下 下 疋 足）	
10	复	ノ ᄂ 占 户 复	
11	詞	言	
		司（ㄱ ㄱ 司）	
12	彙	ク タ 彑 彖 彙	
13	語	言	
		吾	五
			口
14	法	氵	
		去	
15	进		
16	城	土	
		成（厂 万 成 成 成）	

Lesson 28

生詞　Shēngcí　New Words

1.	开始	(动)	kāishǐ	to start, to begin
2.	住	(动)	zhù	to live, to dwell
3.	上(課)	(动)	shàng(kè)	to go to class, to attend class
4.	字	(名)	zì	character
5.	…的时候兒		…dēshíhòur	when…, at the time of
6.	下(課)	(动)	xià(kè)	the class is over, after class
7.	从…起		cóng…qǐ	since…, from the time of
8.	上(月)	(形)	shàng(yuè)	last month, ultimo
9.	从…到…		cóng…dào…	from…to…
10.	已經	(副)	yǐjīng	already
11.	节	(量)	jié	(a measure word)
12.	課	(名)	kè	lesson, class
13.	翻譯	(动、名)	fānyì	to translate, to interpret translation, interpretation, interpreter
14.	特别	(形)	tèbié	special, particular
15.	帮助	(动)	bāngzhù	to help
16.	教室	(名)	jiàoshì	classroom
17.	休息	(动)	xiūxī	rest, to take a rest

語法 Yǔfǎ Grammar

28.1 The Structural Particle 的 (2) We have already learned that when a noun, pronoun or adjective is used to make up an adjective modifier, it is necessary to use the structural particle 的 to join the adjective modifier and the central word together (15.1). Here we shall discuss those adjective modifiers that are made up of verbs, verbal constructions, or subject-predicate constructions (clauses). First of all, let us see how a verb becomes an adjective modifier. e. g.

1. 这本 字典 很 好, 买 的 人 很 多.
   Zhèiběn zìdiǎn hěn hǎo, mǎi dě rén hěn duō.

   This dictionary is very good, and many people buy it (LIT.: buy PARTICLE people very many).

The word 买 in the above example is a simple verb used as adjective modifier. Now let us see how verbal constructions become adjective modifiers. e. g.

2. 上星期 来 的 学生 开始 学习 了.
   Shàngxīngqī lái dě xuéshěng kāishǐ xuéxí lě.

   The student who came last week (LIT.: last week come PARTICLE student) has begun to study.

3. 他 是 从 城里 来 的 那个 同志.
   Tā shì cóng chénglǐ lái dě nèige tóngzhì.

   He is that comrade who came from the city. (LIT.: He is from city-in come PARTICLE that comrade.)

4. 来得 早 的 人 都 在 前边兒.
   Láidě zǎo dě rén dōu zài qiánbiānr.

   All the people who came early are in the front.

5. 她 是 教 語法 的 先生.
   Tā shì jiāo yǔfǎ dě xiānshěng.

   She is the teacher who teaches grammar.

Here, 上星期来 is an adj. modifier composed of a verb and its adverbial modifier, 从城里来 is an adjective modifier composed of a verb and a prepositional construction (phrase) modifying the verb, 来得早 is an adj. modifier composed of a verb and its complement, and 敎語法 is an adj. modifier composed of a verb and its object. Although all the above adj. modifiers are composed of different constructions, yet, the one common feature is that in each of them the verb is used as the main element. Therefore, they are all verbal constructions used as adj. modifiers.

Last of all, let us see how subject-predicate constructions become adj. modifiers. Such modifiers may be divided into two kinds:

(1) The construction in which the predicate is composed mainly of an adjective. e. g.

6. 中文 不 好 的 人 不 会 用 这本
   Zhōngwén bù hǎo dě rén bú huì yòng zhèiběn
   字典.
   zìdiǎn.

   Those who are not good in Chinese (LIT.: Chinese-language not good PARTICLE people) do not know how to use this dictionary.

7. 他 是 一个 工作 积極的 同志.
   Tā shì yígě gōngzuò jījídě tóngzhì.

   He is a comrade who works enthusiastically.

中文不好 and 工作积極 are subject-predicate constructions used as adjective modifiers and the adjectives 好 and 积極 are predicates.

(2) The construction in which the predicate is composed mainly of a verb. e. g.

8. 我 喜欢 他 买 的 那本 書.
   Wǒ xǐhuǎn tā mǎi dě nèiběn shū.

   I like that book he bought. (LIT.: I like he bought PARTICLE that book.)

9. 他們　復習　先生　講　的　語法.
　　Tāmén　fùxí　xiānshēng jiǎng　dé　yǔfǎ.

They reviewed the grammar which the teacher explained (lectured).

他买 and 先生講 are all subject-predicate constructions used as adjective modifiers, and the verbs 买 and 講 are predicates. Notice: such constructions cannot be used independently as complete sentences.

Besides, there is another kind of subject-predicate construction that is complete in meaning by itself, where the verb may or may not carry an object. It is a complete sentence by itself. e. g.

10. <u>他　學習</u>　的　那本　中文　書　是
　　　Tā　xuéxí　dé　nèibēn　zhōngwén　shū　shì

他們的　先生　寫的.
tāmēndē　xiānshēng　xiědē.

That Chinese book he is studying was written by their teacher. (LIT.: He studies PARTICLE that Chinese book is their teacher wrote one.)

11. 哪兒　是　<u>他們　上　課</u>　的　地方?
　　　Nǎr　shì　tāmén　shàng　kè　dé　dìfǎng?

Where do they attend class? (LIT.: Where is they attend class PARTICLE place?)

In all the above sentences, the structural particle 的 has to be inserted between the adjective modifiers and the central words.

When the central words are clearly understood from the context, all the above central words modified by adjective modifiers can be omitted. e. g.

12. 他們　都　在　那兒: <u>説 話</u>　的　是
　　　Tāmén　dōu　zài　nàr: shuō huà　dé　shì

先生, <u>寫　字</u>　的　是　学生.
xiānshēng, xiě　zì　dé　shì　xuéshēng.

They are all there: the one talking is the teacher, the ones writing characters are the students.

13. 我　給　他　的　是　一本　書.
Wǒ　gěi　tā　de　shì　yìběn　shū.

It was a book that I gave him. (LIT.: I gave him PAR-
TICLE is one book.)

In example 12, 人 has been omitted and in example 13 东西
has been omitted.

28.2 ...的时候兒　This is a very common construction
eqivalent to the English "when" or "at the time of...". In
general, it is placed after a word or a complicated construction
used as adverbial modifier. e. g.

14. 工作　的　时候兒，他　一定　好好兒地
Gōngzuò de shíhòur, tā yídìng hǎohāorde

工作.
gōngzuò.

When he works, he certainly works very well.

15. 作　練習　的　时候兒，他　写　汉字
Zuò liànxí de shíhòur, tā xiě hànzì

写得　很　清楚.
xiěde hěn qīngchǔ.

When he does his exercises, he writes the characters
very clearly.

16. 我　回　宿舍　的　时候兒，他　还
Wǒ huí sùshè de shíhòur, tā hái

沒　下　課　呢!
méi xià kè ně!

When I returned to the dormitory, he was not yet
finished with his class.

28.3 从...起　It is also a common construction used as
adverbial modifier of time. e. g.

17. 他們　从　上月　起　学習　中文.
Tāmen cóng shàngyuè qǐ xuéxí zhōngwén.

They have been studying Chinese since last month.

18. 我們 从 学習 語法 起, 作了 很
Wǒmén cóng xuéxí yǔfǎ qǐ, zuòlė hěn

多 練習 了.
duō liànxí lė.

Since we studied the grammar, we have been doing many exercises.

19. 从 我 認識 他 起, 我們 常常
Cóng wǒ rènshì tā qǐ, wǒmén chángcháng

一起 学習.
yìqǐ xuéxí.

Since I met him, we have often studied together.

From the above examples, we see that we may either insert a word or a complicated construction into this construction.

28.4 从...到... This is also a common construction used as adverbial modifier of time. e. g.

20. 我們 从 七点半 到 十点半 学習.
Wǒmén cóng qīdiǎnbàn dào shídiǎnbàn xuéxí.

We studied from 7:30 to 10:30.

21. 他 从 一九五二年 到 一九五五年
Tā cóng yījiǔwǔèrnián dào yījiǔwǔwǔnián

在 北京 大学 工作.
zài Běijīng Dàxué gōngzuò.

He worked at Peking University from 1952 to 1955.

But, it may also be used as adjective modifier indicating limit or scope. e. g.

22. 星期六 我們 复習 从 星期一 到
Xīngqīliù wǒmén fùxí cóng xīngqīyī dào

星期五 的 語法.
xīngqīwǔ dė yǔfǎ.

On Saturday we reviewed the grammar from Monday's to Friday's (grammar).

課文 Kèwén Text
SIDE SIX, BAND FIVE

I

上星期 我 看了 你 給 我 的
Shàngxīngqī wǒ kànle nǐ gěi wǒ de

那本 画报. 你 給 我 的 那本 画报
nèiběn huàbào. Nǐ gěi wǒ de nèiběn huàbào

很 有意思, 不 会 中文 的 人 也
hěn yǒuyìsi, bú huì zhōngwén de rén yě

能 看 那本 画报.
néng kàn nèiběn huàbào.

Last week I read that picture news magazine you gave
me. That picture news magazine you gave me is very
interesting; even people who don't know Chinese can
read that picture news magazine.

II

他們 从 上星期 起, 已經 开始 学-
Tāmén cóng shàngxīngqī qǐ, yǐjīng kāishǐ xué-

習 了. 从 八点 (过) 五分 到 十一点
xí le. Cóng bādiǎn (guò) wǔfēn dào shíyīdiǎn

四十分, 他們 有 四节 课. 上 课 的
sìshífēn, tāmén yǒu sìjié kè. Shàng kè de

时候兒, 先生 説 中文 説得 很 慢、很
shíhòur, xiānshēng shuō zhōngwén shuōde hěn màn、hěn

清楚, 他們 都 能 懂 先生 説 的 話.
qīngchǔ, tāmén dōu néng dǒng xiānshēng shuō de huà.

复習 的 时候兒, 作 翻譯 工作 的 同志
Fùxí de shíhòur, zuò fānyì gōngzuò de tóngzhì

还 特別 帮助 他們.
hái tèbié bāngzhù tāmén.

Since last week they have already begun to study.
From five after eight to eleven-forty they have four
classes. During the classes, the teacher speaks Chinese
very slowly and clearly, and they all are able to under-

stand everything the teacher says. When they review, the comrade who does translation (work) gives them special help also.

III

从 苏联 来 的 学生 都 在 这个
Cóng Sūlián lái de xuéshēng dōu zài zhèige

宿舍里 住. 他們 上 課 的 教室 在
sùshèli zhù. Tāmén shàng kè de jiàoshì zài

宿舍 旁边兒. 下 課 的 时候兒, 他們
sùshè pángbiānr. Xià kè de shíhòur, tāmén

都 在 教室 外边兒 休息. 休息 的
dōu zài jiàoshì wàibiānr xiūxi. Xiūxi de

时候兒, 先生 看 画报, 学生 唱 歌兒.
shíhòur, xiānshēng kàn huàbào, xuéshēng chàng gēr.

先生 都 喜欢 看 "人民 画报", 学生
Xiānshēng dōu xǐhuán kàn "Rénmín Huàbào", xuéshēng

都 喜欢 唱 張 同志 教 他們 的
dōu xǐhuán chàng Zhāng tóngzhì jiāo tāmén de

中文 歌兒.
zhōngwén gēr.

All the students from the Soviet Union live in this dormitory. The classroom where they meet is next to the dormitory. When the class is over, they all rest outside the classroom. During the rest period, the teacher reads picture news magazines and the students sing. The teachers like to read "The People's Picture Magazine" and the students like to sing Chinese songs which Comrade Chāng taught them.

課外練習 Kèwài liànxí Home Work

1) Translate the following sentences into Chinese:

(1) Those who want to see the film have already gone to the city.

(2) The newspaper he is now reading (literally to see) is yesterday's.

(3) Students **who are good** in English may read the English magazines.

(4) The place **where we are resting** is beside the auditorium.

2) Copy the following sentences and fill the blanks with either 得 or 的:

(5) 学习＿＿多 的 学生 应该 帮助 学习得 少＿＿学生.

(6) 我 同屋 买＿＿东西 都 在 桌子上.

(7) 我 写 从前 学＿＿词彙, 写＿＿快; 我 写 今天 学＿＿词彙, 写＿＿.慢

汉字表 Hànzì biǎo Chinese Characters

1	开	二 于 开	
2	始	女	
		台	厶
			口
3	住	亻	
		主 (丶 一 二 于 主)	
4	課	言	
		果 (曰 旦 果)	
5	到	至	
		刂	
6	已	乛 ⊐ 已	

7	經	糸		
		巠 （一 て 灭 巠 巠）		
8	节	丷		
		卩 （フ 卩）		
9	翻	番	釆 （ノ く 丷 乎 釆 釆）	
			田	
		羽		
10	譯	言		
		睪	四	
			幸 （土 十 圥 幸 幸）	
11	特	牛 （ノ 二 牛 牛）		
		寺	土	
			寸	
12	別	另	口	
			力	
		刂		
13	帮	邦 （一 二 三 丰 邦）		
		巾		
14	助	且 （丨 冂 月 且 且）		
		力		

15	室	宀
		至
16	休	亻
		木
17	息	自 (丿 自)
		心

Lesson 29

生詞 Shēngcí New Words

SIDE SIX, BAND SIX

1.	还是	(連) háishì	or
2.	每	(代) měi	each, every
3.	生詞	(名) shēngcí	new word
4.	小説兒	(名) xiǎoshuōr [本]	novel
5.	借	(动) jiè	to lend, to borrow
6.	想	(动、能动) xiǎng	to think, to want, to intend
7.	还	(动) huán	to return, to give back
8.	可以	(能动) kěyǐ	may
9.	謝謝	xièxiè	to thank, thanks
10.	問	(动) wèn	to ask, to inquire
11.	問題	(名) wèntí	question, problem
12.	必須	(能动) bìxū	must, have to
13.	回答	(动、名) huídá	to answer, to reply
14.	对	(形) duì	right, correct
15.	告訴	(动) gàosù	to tell, to inform
16.	方法	(名) fāngfǎ	way, method

語法 Yǔfǎ Grammar

29.1 **The Inversion of Object** We know already that in Chinese the general word order of the sentence with a verbal predicate is:

(Adj. modifier) Subject — (Adverbial modifier) Verb — (Adj. modifier) Object

But the object can be put before the subject under certain conditions. Here we shall introduce two kinds of sentences with inverted object:

(1) In a sentence in which the predicate is comparatively complicated (or when the object consists of several words), the sentence becomes more compact and clearer in meaning, if the object is transposed to the beginning of the sentence. e. g.

1. 中文　書　我　朋友　看得　很　快.
Zhōngwén shū wǒ péngyǒu kànde hěn kuài.

My friend reads Chinese books very quickly. ("Chinese books" comes first)

2. 先生　説　的　話　我　聽得　很　清-
Xiānsheng shuō de huà wǒ tīngde hěn qīng-

楚.
chǔ.

I (generally) hear very clearly what the teacher says. (LIT.: Teacher says PARTICLE speech I hear PARTICLE very clearly.)

In each of the above two sentences, there is a complement of degree. If the objects are not transposed, the verbs have to be reduplicated. (e. g. 我朋友看中文書, 看得很快 and 我聽先生的話, 聽得很清楚). For the sake of compactness, the object is always put at the beginning of a sentence.

When the object is a compound object or in the plural form, the adverb 都 has to be used before the predicate. e. g.

3. 練習里的　汉字　他　都　写得　很
Liànxílide hànzì tā dōu xiěde hěn

好看.
hǎokàn.

He (generally) writes (all) the characters in the exercises very beautifully.

4. 我　买　的　杂誌　你　都　能　看.
Wǒ　mǎi　dê　zázhì　nǐ　dōu　néng　kàn.
You may read (all) the magazines I bought.

(2) In order to stress the object in a sentence, we can transpose the object to the beginning of a sentence. e. g.

5. 这个　月的　人民　画报　我　已經
Zhèigê　yuèdê　Rénmín　Huàbào　wǒ　yǐjing

看　了.
kàn　lê.
I have already read this month's "People's Picture Magazine."

6. 那个　新　同志的　名字　我　不　知道.
Nèigê　xīn　tóngzhìdê　míngzî　wǒ　bù　zhīdào.
I don't know that new comrade's name.

The parallel elements in a sentence are always stressed. If they happen to be two objects, we may transpose them to the beginning of the sentence. e. g.

7. 新　杂誌　我　买,　旧　杂誌　我　不
Xīn　zázhì　wǒ　mǎi,　jiù　zázhì　wǒ　bù

买.
mǎi.
I buy new magazines, I don't buy old magazines.

8. 昨天的　語法　他　懂,　今天的　(語法)
Zuótiândê　yǔfǎ　tā　dǒng,　jīntiândê　(yǔfǎ)

他　也　懂.
tā　yě　dǒng.
He understands yesterday's grammar, and he understands today's (grammar) also.

The parallel elements are joined together sometimes for contrast (as in example 7) and sometimes according to the sequence of time (as in example 8). In the latter case, the adverb 也 is always used. But a compound object may be used instead of the parallel construction, if it is a kind that is based on the sequence of time. e. g.

9. 昨天的　語法　和　今天的　語法　他
   Zuótiānde　yǔfǎ　hé　jīntiānde　yǔfǎ　tā

   都　懂.
   dōu　dǒng.

   He understands (both) yesterday's grammar and today's grammar.

Note: When the compound object is transposed to the beginning of the sentence, the adverb 都 has to be added before the predicate.

29.2   The Interrogative Sentence (4)   The fourth kind of the interrogative sentence contains two alternative questions represented by the construction (compound conjunction) (还是) …还是…… The construction (还是)…还是 should be placed before the elements concerning which the questions are asked. e. g.

10. (还是)　你　来,　还是　她　来?
    (Hái shì)　nǐ　lái,　háishì　tā　lái?

    Are you coming or is she coming?

11. 你　(还是)　来,　还是　不　来?
    Nǐ　(háishì)　lái,　háishì　bù　lái?

    Are you coming or not (coming)?

In example 10, we wish to know "who is coming", putting 还是 before the subject of each clause; in example 11, we wish to know whether "you will come or not", with 还是 before the compound predicate.

29.3 每 includes all the individual members or elements of a group of persons or things. Two points should be noticed in using the word 每:

(1) It is a demonstrative pronoun and cannot be directly used with a noun. There should be a measure word. e. g.

12. 每个　学生　都　很　努力　学习.
    Měigè　xuéshēng　dōu　hěn　nǔlì　xuéxí.

    Every (OR: Each) student studies very diligently.

13. 每張　桌子　都　很　干淨.
Měizhāng　zhuōzǐ　dōu　hěn　gānjìng.
Every table is very clean.

However, some nouns have the function of measure words, so they can be directly used with the word 每. e. g.

14. 我們　每天　八点　过　五分　上　課.
Wǒmen　měitiān　bādiǎn　guò　wǔfēn　shàng　kè.
We start class every day at 8:05.

15. 每課　有　十五个　生詞.
Měikè　yǒu　shíwǔgè　shēngcí.
There are fifteen new words in every lesson.

(2) When the word 每 is used as adjective modifier of the subject, the adverb 都 is always placed before the predicate. e. g.

16. 每个　学生　都　作了　練習　了.
Měigè　xuéshēng　dōu　zuòle　liànxí　le.
Every student has done the exercises.

17. 每(个)　人　都　应該　会　用　那
Měi(gè)　rén　dōu　yīnggāi　huì　yòng　nèi-
本　字典.
běn　zìdiǎn.
Everybody ought to be able to use that dictionary.

But 都 may also be omitted. When such is the case 每 takes on almost the same meaning as 一. e. g.

18. 每年　有　十二个　月.
Měinián　yǒu　shíèrgè　yuè.
There are twelve months in a (every) year.

19. 每个　学生　应該　有　两个　本子.
Měigè　xuéshēng　yīnggāi　yǒu　liǎnggè　běnzǐ.
A (Every) student ought to have two notebooks.

課文 Kèwén Text

SIDE SIX, BAND SIX

I

(a₁) 这 两本 小说兒 是 誰的? 是
Zhèi liǎngběn xiǎoshuōr shì shéidė? Shì

你的, 还是 張 同志的?
nǐdė, háishì Zhāng tóngzhìdė?

Who owns these two novels? Are they yours or Comrade Chāng's?

(b₁) 这本 中文的 是 張 同志的, 那本
Zhèiběn zhōngwéndė shì Zhāng tóngzhìdė, nèiběn

俄文的 是 我 在 圖書館 借 的.
èwéndė shì wǒ zài túshūguǎn jiè dė.

This one in Chinese is Comrade Chāng's, that one in Russian is the one I borrowed from the library.

(a₂) 两本 你 都 看 了 嗎?
Liǎngběn nǐ dōu kàn lė má?

Have you read them both?

(b₂) 对 了, 两本 都 看 了.
Duì lė, liǎngběn dōu kàn lė.

Right, I have read them both.

(a₃) 哪本 好? 还是 中文的 有意思,
Něiběn hǎo? Háishì zhōngwéndė yǒuyìsì,

还是 俄文的 有意思?
háishì èwéndė yǒuyìsì?

Which one is good? Is the Chinese one or the Russian one interesting?

(b₃) 都　有意思.　我　都　喜欢.
Dōu　yǒuyìsi.　Wǒ　dōu　xǐhuǎn.

你　想　不　想　看?
Nǐ　xiǎng　bù　xiǎng　kàn?

They're both interesting. I like them both. Do you want to read them?

(a₄) 俄文的　想　看,　中文的　我　还
Èwéndě　xiǎng　kàn,　zhōngwéndě　wǒ　hái

不　懂　呢!　你　哪天　还　这本
bù　dǒng　ně!　Nǐ　něitiān　huán　zhèiběn

俄文的?
èwéndě?

I want to read the Russian one; I wouldn't understand the Chinese one yet. On what day are you returning this Russian one?

(b₄) 下星期　还.　你　可以　在　这个
Xiàxīngqī　huán.　Nǐ　kěyǐ　zài　zhèigě

星期里　看.
xīngqīlǐ　kàn.

Next week. You may read it this week.

(a₅) 謝謝,　我　看了　就　还　你.
Xièxiě,　wǒ　kànlě　jiù　huán　nǐ.

Thank you, I'll read it and then return it to you.

II

(a₆) 你們　每天　上　几节　課?
Nǐmén　měitiān　shàng　jǐjié　kè?

How many classes do you have every day?

(b₆) 每天　四节.
Měitiān　sìjié.
Four a day.

(a₇) 每天　都　上　四节　課　嗎?
Měitiān　dōu　shàng　sìjié　kè　må?
You have four classes a day?

(b₇) 对　了，我們　現在　每天　都　上
Duì　lě,　wǒměn　xiànzài　měitiān　dōu　shàng
四节　課，星期六　也　上　四节　課.
sìjié　kè,　xīngqīliù　yě　shàng　sìjié　kè.
Yes, now we have four classes a day, even on Saturday.

(a₈) 上　課　的　时候兒，先生　問　你
Shàng　kè　dě　shíhǒur,　xiānshěng　wèn　nǐ-
們　問題　嗎?
měn　wèntí　må?
During the class, does the teacher ask you questions?

(b₈) 問，他　每天　都　問.
Wèn,　tā　měitiān　dōu　wèn.
Yes, every day.

(a₉) 每个　学生　他　都　問　嗎?
Měigě　xuéshěng　tā　dōu　wèn　må?
Does he question every student?

(b₉) 每个　学生　他　都　問.每人　都
Měigě　xuéshěng　tā　dōu　wèn.　Měirén　dōu
必須　回答.
bìxū　huídá.
He questions every student. Everyone must answer.

(a₁₀) 先生的　問題　你們　都　回答得
Xiānshēngdě　wèntí　nǐmên　dōu　huídádê

对　嗎?
duì　mǎ?

Do you answer all the teacher's questions correctly?

(b₁₀) 回答得　不　对　的　时候兒,　先-
Huídádê　bú　duì　dê　shíhôur,　xiān-

生　就　告訴　我們.　这　是　練習
shêng　jiù　gàosû　wǒmên.　Zhèi　shì　liànxí

的　好　方法.
dê　hǎo　fāngfǎ.

When we don't answer correctly, then the teacher tells us (so). This is a good method of practice.

課外練習　Kèwài liànxí　Home Work

1) Re-write the following interrogative sentences with (还是) … 还是:

(1) 你　什么　时候兒　(今天, 明天)　还
他　这本　字典?

(2) 他　唱　的　是　什么 (俄文的, 中文的)
歌兒?

2) Make sentences with each of the following groups of words:

(3) 每　小説兒

(4) 每　年

(3) Change the following into sentences with inverted objects:

(5) 他 回答 先生 問 的 两个
問題 回答得 特別 清楚.

(6) 先生 已經 告訴 我們 复習
詞彙 的 方法 了, 还 没有 告訴
我們 复習 語法 的 方法 呢!

汉字表 Hànzì biǎo Chinese Characters

1	每	ノ 亠 仁 勺 每 每 每
2	借	亻
		昔（一 十 艹 芷 昔）
3	想	相　木
		目
		心
4	可	
5	謝	言
		射　身（ノ 亻 竹 身 身 身 身）
		寸
6	問	
7	題	
8	必	丶 心 心 必 必

9	須	彡
		頁
10	答	竹
		合
11	告	ノ 丿 牛 坓 告
12	訴	言
		斥 （斤 斥）

Lesson 30

語法复習　Yǔfǎ fùxí　Review

30.1 The Past Tense and the Perfective Aspect　　Time and aspect are two different things. One of the characteristic features of the Chinese language is that the morphology of a verb is not determined by time but by aspect. Let us clarify this problem by making a comparison between the past tense and the perfective aspect.

In Chinese, time is generally expressed by an adverbial modifier of time; so a past action is always shown by an adverbial modifier made up of a word or word group expressing some past time. e. g.

1. 我們　<u>从前</u>　常常　唱　中国　歌兒.
   Wǒmén　cóngqián　chángcháng　chàng　Zhōngguó　gēr.
   In the past (Before) we often sang Chinese songs.

2. <u>一九五六年</u>　他們　在　这个　工厂
   Yījiǔwǔliùnián　tāmén　zài　zhèige　gōngchǎng
   工作.
   gōngzuò.
   They worked in this factory in 1956.

唱中国歌兒　and　工作　are all past actions, the time of the actions being shown by the words 从前 and 1956 年. But the verbs themselves are not inflected. It is because verbs in Chinese do not change in form according to the change of time. Hence, we must never put the suffix 了 after verbs, when the actions are in the past.

In Chinese, the inflection of a verb is determined by the different state of an action. An action may be in its progressive, continuous or complete state, and the word 了 is the suffix indicating the perfective aspect. But we must pay attention to the fact that the suffix 了 is used only when we wish to lay stress on the completion of an action. When we have no wish to emphasize the completion of an action in the past, there is no need to use this suffix.

30.2 Time of Action of the Perfective Aspect   As mentioned above, the aspect of an action is only determined by the state of the action. Therefore, whether the action is in the past or in the future, it may have different aspects. Sentences of the perfective aspect (we have already learned these) can be classified into two kinds:

(1) When the sentence contains only one action in the past. e. g.

3. 昨天　我　看了　一本　小説兒.
　　Zuótiān　wǒ　kànlě　yìběn　xiǎoshuōr.
　　Yesterday I read a novel.

(2) When there are two actions in the sentence, in general, the second action takes place only after the completion of the first action. So far as time is concerned, such sentences may be subdivided into two kinds:

a) Both actions take place in the past time. e. g.

4. 昨天　他　下了　課,　很　快地　就
　　Zuótiān　tā　xiàlě　kè,　hěn　kuàidě　jiù

去　圖書館　了.
qù　túshūguǎn　lě.

　　Yesterday, after his class was over, he went to the library very quickly.

b) Both actions happen in the future. e. g.

5. 明天　我　下了　課,　就　回　宿舍.
　　Míngtiān　wǒ　xiàlě　kè,　jiù　huí　sùshè.
　　Tomorrow, after my class is over, I shall return to the dormitory.

We may arrive at the conclusion:

(1) In Chinese, the inflection of a verb shows aspect only; time and aspect are entirely two different things— the perfective aspect is not the same as the past tense.

(2) There is perfective aspect in the past time as well as in the future. When we wish to emphasize one future action happening after the completion of another one, the latter should be told by a verb of the perfective aspect.

30.3 不 and 沒有 These two adverbs indicate negation, but 沒有 is only used in the sentence with a verbal predicate.

Here we shall deal with the negative forms of the sentence with a verbal predicate:

(1) 不 is used under the following conditions:

(a) All the customary or habitual actions, whatever the time may be, are negated by 不. e. g.

6. 從前　他　不　跳　舞.
　 Cóngqián　tā　bú　tiào　wú.
　 Formerly he didn't dance.

7. 這個　先生　不　教　我們,　那個
　 Zhèige　xiānshēng　bù　jiāo　wǒmen,　nèige
　 先生　教　我們.
　 xiānshēng　jiāo　wǒmen.
　 This teacher is not our instructor (does not teach us), that teacher is our instructor (teaches us).

(b) 不 is used to negate all future actions. e. g.

8. 星期日　我們　休息,　不　工作.
　 Xīngqīrì　wǒmen　xiūxi,　bù　gōngzuò.
　 On Sunday we rest, we do not work.

9. 下星期　他　不　進　城.
　 Xiàxīngqī　tā　bú　jìn　chéng.
　 Next week he will not go into the city.

Only when we wish to stress an action that is not yet completed, we use 沒有. e. g.

10. 我　必須　在　明天　还　没　有　上
　　 Wǒ　bìxū　zài　míngtiān　hái　méi　yǒu　shàng

　　 課　的　时候　練習　这些　汉字.
　　 kè　dě　shíhǒur　liànxí　zhèixiē　hànzì.

Tomorrow I must practice these characters before the class begins. (LIT.: I must at tomorrow still not have attend class PARTICLE time practice these characters.)

(c) 不 is used to negate intention or wish regardless of the time. e. g.

11. 休息　的　时候兒　他　看　画报, 不
　　 Xiūxi　dě　shíhǒur　tā　kàn　huàbào,　bú

　　 唱歌兒.
　　 chànggěr.

In the rest period he reads picture news magazines, he does not sing.

12. 他　不　喜欢　这个　电影,　他　不
　　 Tā　bù　xǐhuān　zhèigě　diànyǐng,　tā　bú

　　 看.
　　 kàn.

He does not like this film, he will not see it.

(d) 不 is used before optative verbs or verbs implying mental states. e. g.

13. 开始　学習　的　时候兒,　我　不　会
　　 Kāishǐ　xuéxí　dě　shíhǒur,　wǒ　bú　huì

　　 說　中国　話.
　　 shuō　Zhōngguó　huà.

When I began studying, I was not able to speak Chinese.

14. 他　没　有　告訴　我,　我　不　知道.
　　 Tā　méi　yǒu　gàosǔ　wǒ,　wǒ　bù　zhīdào.

He didn't tell me, I don't know.

(2) 没有 is used to show that a certain action has not happened. e. g.

15. 我　同屋　还　沒　有　回　宿舍　呢!
　　Wǒ　tóngwū　hái　méi　yǒu　huí　sùshè　ně!

My roommate has not yet returned to the dormitory.

16. 我　只　借了　画报,　沒　有　借　小
　　Wǒ　zhǐ　jièlě　huàbào,　méi　yǒu　jiè　xiǎo-
説兒.
shuōr.

I borrowed only a picture news magazine, I did not borrow a novel.

課文　Kèwén　Text

SIDE SIX, BAND SEVEN

(a₁)　昨天　是　星期日,　您　作　什么　了?
　　Zuótiǎn　shì　xīngqīrì,　nín　zuò　shénmǒ　lě?

Yesterday was Sunday; what did you (formal) do?

(b₁)　我　进　城　了. 我　看了　一个　朋友.
　　Wǒ　jìn　chéng　lě.　Wǒ　kànlě　yígě　péngyǒu.

I went into the city (into town). I saw a friend.

(a₂)　您的　这个　朋友　是　作　什么　工
　　Níndě　zhèigě　péngyǒu　shì　zuò　shénmǒ　gōng-
作　的,　您　能　告訴　我　嗎?
zuò　dě,　nín　néng　gàosǔ　wǒ　mǎ?

Can you (formal) tell me what work this friend of yours does?

(b₂)　他　在　学校里　教　書.
　　Tā　zài　xuéxiàolǐ　jiāo　shū.

He is a schoolteacher.

(a₃) 他 教 什么?
Tā jiāo shénmǒ?

What does he teach?

(b₃) 他 教 俄文. 我 朋友 教 俄文
Tā jiāo èwén. Wǒ péngyǒu jiāo èwén

的 方法 很 好, 学生 都 学得
dě fāngfǎ hěn hǎo, xuéshēng dōu xuédě

很 快. 他們 从 九月 起 开始
hěn kuài. Tāmēn cóng jiǔyuè qǐ kāishǐ

学習, 已經 会 说、 会 写 了.
xuéxí, yǐjīng huì shuō, huì xiě lě.

He teaches Russian. My friend's method of teaching
Russian is very good; his students learn very quickly.
They started to learn in September and can already
speak and write.

(a₄) 他們 每天 都 有 课 嗎?
Tāmēn měitiān dōu yǒu kè mǎ?

Do they have classes every day?

(b₄) 都 有. 从 星期一 到 星期六
Dōu yǒu. Cóng xīngqīyī dào xīngqīliù

他 每天 講 两节 語法. 你
tā měitiān jiǎng liǎngjié yǔfǎ. Nǐ

星期日 进 城 了 嗎?
xīngqīrì jìn chéng lě mǎ?

Yes. Every day from Monday to Saturday he gives two
grammar lessons. Did you go into the city on Sunday?

(a₅) 没 有, 我 在 宿舍 看 書 了.
Méi yǒu, wǒ zài sùshè kàn shū lě.

我 星期六 从 朋友 那兒 借了
Wǒ xīngqīliù cóng péngyǒu nàr jièlě

一本　　翻譯　　小説兒,　星期日　　一天
yìběn　　fānyì　　xiǎoshuōr,　xīngqīrì　　yìtiān

我　都　看　小説兒　了.
wǒ　dōu　kàn　xiǎoshuōr　lě.

No, I read in the dormitory. On Saturday I borrowed a translated novel from a friend, and on Sunday (in one day) I read the whole novel.

(b₅) 这本　　小説兒　　写得　　怎么样?
Zhèiběn　xiǎoshuōr　xiědě　zěnmòyàng?

How is the writing in this novel?

(a₆) 这本　　小説兒　　写得　很　好.　你　要
Zhèiběn　xiǎoshuōr　xiědě　hěn　hǎo.　Nǐ　yào

不　要　看?
bú　yào　kàn?

Very good. Do you want to read it?

(b₆) 我　要　看.　下星期　还,　可以　吗?
Wǒ　yào　kàn.　Xiàxīngqī　huán,　kěyǐ　mǎ?

Yes. I'll return it next week. May I?

(a₇) 可以,　你　可以　慢慢兒地　看.
Kěyǐ,　nǐ　kěyǐ　mànmānrdě　kàn.

我　不　一定　现在　还　他.
Wǒ　bù　yídìng　xiànzài　huán　tā.

Yes. You may read it (very) slowly. I'm certainly not returning it to him now.

(b₇) 好.
Hǎo.
Good.

Vocabulary

(The words are arranged in the order of the phonetic alphabet, and the number after each word represents the number of the lesson in which the word appears.)

B

bā	八	(数)	bā	eight	22
bǎ	把	(量)	bǎ	(a measure word)	17
bàn	半	(数)	bàn	half	22
bāng	帮助	(动)	bāngzhù	to help	28
bào	报	(名)	bào	newspaper	13
běi	北京	(名)	Běijīng	Peking	14
	北京大学	(名)	Běijīng-dàxué	Peking University	17
běn	本	(量)	běn	(a measure word)	14
	本子	(名)	běnzi 〔本〕	note-book	16
bì	必须	(能动)	bìxū	must, have to	29
bù	不	(副)	bù	not, no	13

C

chà	差	(动)	chà	less	25
cháng	長	(形)	cháng	long	15
	常常	(副)	chángcháng	often	21
chàng	唱(歌兒)	(动)	chàng(gēr)	to sing (song)	21
chéng	城	(名)	chéng	city, town	27
cí	詞彙	(名)	cíhuì	vocabulary	27

cóng	从	(介)	cóng	from	20
	从前	(副)	cóngqián	in the past, formerly	27
	从...起		cóng...qǐ	since, from the time of	28
	从...到...		cóng...dào...	from... to...	28

D

dà	大	(形)	dà	big, large	14
dē	的	(助)	dē	(a structural particle)	15
	地	(助)	dē	(a structural particle)	20
	得	(助)	dē	(a structural particle)	21
	...的时候儿		...dēshíhóur	when, at the time of	28
dì	地方	(名)	dìfāng	place	23
diǎn	点(鐘)	(名)	diǎn(zhōng)	o'clock	25
diàn	电影	(名)	diànyǐng	film, moving picture	20
dōng	东西	(名)	dōngxi	thing	26
dǒng	懂	(动)	dǒng	to understand, to know	19
dōu	都	(副)	dōu	all	17
duǎn	短	(形)	duǎn	short	15
duì	对了		duìlê	yes, that is right	17
	对	(形)	duì	right, correct	29
duō	多	(形)	duō	many, much	14
	多少	(数)	duōshǎo	how many, how much	22

E

| è | 俄文 | (名) | èwén | the Russian language | 15 |
| èr | 二 | (数) | èr | two | 22 |

F

| fān | 翻譯 | (动、名) | fānyì | to translate, to interpret translation, interpretation, interpreter | 28 |
| fāng | 方法 | (名) | fāngfǎ | way, method | 29 |

| fēn | 分 | (名) | fēn | minute | 25 |
| fù | 复习 | (动) | fùxí | to review | 27 |

G

gān	干淨	(形)	gānjing	clean	15
gāng	鋼笔	(名)	gāngbǐ 〔枝〕	pen	17
gāo	高兴	(形)	gāoxìng	glad, happy	20
gào	告訴	(动)	gàosu	to tell, to inform	29
gē	歌兒	(名)	gēr	song	21
gè	个	(量)	gè	(a measure word)	14
gěi	給	(动)	gěi	to give	16
gēn	跟	(介)	gēn	with, after	20
gōng	工作	(动、名)	gōngzuò	to work, work	16
	工厂	(名)	gōngchǎng	factory	23
guó	国	(名)	guó	country	19
guò	过	(动)	guò	to pass, past	25

H

hái	还	(副)	hái	also, too, still	26
	还是	(連)	háishì	or	29
hàn	汉字	(名)	hànzì	Chinese character	21
hǎo	好	(形)	hǎo	good, well	14
	好看	(形)	hǎokàn	good-looking	26
hào	号	(名)	hào	day, number	25
hé	和	(連)	hé	and	17
hēi	黑板	(名)	hēibǎn	blackboard	15
hěn	很	(副)	hěn	very	14
hòu	后边兒	(名)	hòubiānr	back, the following	23
huà	画报	(名)	huàbào 〔本〕	pictorial	17
	話	(名)	huà	words, speech	21

huán	还	(动)	huán	to return, to give back	29
huí	回	(动)	huí	to go back, to return	27
	回答	(动、名)	huídá	to answer, to reply	29
huì	会	(动)	huì	to know how to do	17
	会	(能动)	huì	can, may	26

J

ji	积极	(形)	jījí	enthusiastic, active	20
jǐ	几	(数)	jǐ	how many, several, a few	22
jiǎng	講	(动)	jiǎng	to explain, to give a lecture on, to tell	27
jiāo	教	(动)	jiāo	to teach	16
jiào	叫	(动)	jiào	to call, to be called	19
	教室	(名)	jiàoshì	classroom	28
jié	节	(量)	jié	(a measure word)	28
jiè	借	(动)	jiè	to lend, to borrow	29
jīn	今天	(名)	jīntiān	today	25
	今年	(名)	jīnnián	this year	25
jìn	进	(动)	jìn	to enter	27
jiù	旧	(形)	jiù	old	14
	就	(副)	jiù	then, at once	27
jù	句子	(名)	jùzi	sentence	27
jué	觉得	(动)	juéde	to feel	26

K

kāi	开始	(动)	kāishǐ	to start, to begin	28
kàn	看	(动)	kàn	to see, to look at	16
kě	可以	(能动)	kěyi	may	29
kè	刻	(名)	kè	a quarter	25
	課	(名)	kè	lesson, class	28
kuài	快	(形)	kuài	quick, fast	21

L

lái	来	(动)	lái	to come	16
lē	了	(尾、助)	lē	(a suffix and a particle)	27
lǐ	里边儿	(名)	lǐbiānr	inside	23
	礼堂	(名)	lǐtáng	auditorium (hall)	23
liàn	練習	(名、动)	liànxí	exercise, to exercise, to practise	22
liǎng	两	(数)	liǎng	two	22
liù	六	(数)	liù	six	22

M

mā	嗎	(助)	mā	(an interrogative particle)	13
mǎi	买	(动)	mǎi	to buy	26
màn	慢	(形)	màn	slow	21
máng	忙	(形)	máng	busy	25
méi	沒	(副)	méi	not	16
	沒关系		méiguānxi	never mind, it doesn't matter	26
měi	每	(代)	měi	each, every	29
míng	名字	(名)	míngzi	name	19
	明天	(名)	míngtiān	tomorrow	27

N

nǎ	哪兒	(代)	nǎr	where	20
	哪里	(代)	nǎli	where	20
nà	那兒	(代)	nàr	there	20
	那里	(代)	nàli	there	20
nē	呢	(助)	nē	(a particle)	27
něi	哪	(代)	něi	which	19
nèi	那	(代)	nèi, nà	that	13

néng	能	(能动) néng	to be able, can	26
nǐ	你	(代) nǐ	you	13
	你們	(代) nǐmén	you	15
nián	年	(名) nián	year	22
niàn	念	(动) niàn	to read	21
nín	您	(代) nín	(the polite form of 你)	13
nǔ	努力	(形) nǔlì	diligent, strenuous	20

P

| páng | 旁边儿 | (名) pángbiānr | side, beside | 23 |
| péng | 朋友 | (名) péngyǒu | friend | 15 |

Q

qī	七	(数) qī	seven	22
qiān	鉛笔	(名) qiānbǐ〔枝〕	pencil	15
qián	前边兒	(名) qiánbiānr	front	23
qīng	清楚	(形) qīngchǔ	clear	27
qù	去	(动) qù	to go	20

R

rén	人	(名) rén	man, person	13
	人民	(名) rénmín	people	19
rèn	認識	(动、名) rènshi	to know, to recognize	26
rì	日	(名) rì	day	25

S

sān	三	(数) sān	three	**14**
shàng	上边兒	(名) shàngbiānr	above	23
	上(星期)	shàng(xīngqī)	last (week)	27
	上(課)	shàng(kè)	to go to class, to attend class	28
	上(月)	shàng(yuè)	last month, ultimo	28
shǎo	少	(形) shǎo	few, little	**14**

shéi	誰	(代)	shéi	who	19
shén	什么	(代)	shénmŏ	what	19
shēng	生詞	(名)	shēngcí	new word	29
shí	十	(數)	shí	ten	22
	时候兒	(名)	shíhòur	time	25
shì	是	(动)	shì	to be	13
shū	書	(名)	shū	book	13
shuō	說(話)	(动)	shuō(huà)	to speak	21
sì	四	(數)	sì	four	22
sū	苏联	(名)	Sūlián	the Soviet Union	19
sù	宿舍	(名)	sùshè	dormitory, hostel	23

T

tā	他	(代)	tā	he, him	13
	他們	(代)	tāmĕn	they, them	15
	她	(代)	tā	she, her	15
	它	(代)	tā	it	15
tài	太	(副)	tài	too	21
tè	特別	(形)	tèbié	special, particular	28
tiān	天	(名)	tiān	day	25
tiào	跳(舞)	(动)	tiào(wŭ)	to dance	21
tīng	听	(动)	tīng	to hear, to listen to	26
tóng	同志	(名)	tóngzhì	comrade	15
	同屋	(名)	tóngwū	room-mate	19
tú	圖書館	(名)	túshūguăn	library	23

W

wài	外边儿	(名)	wàibiānr	outside	23
wăn	晚	(形)	wăn	late	21
wèn	問	(动)	wèn	to ask, to inquire	29
	問題	(名)	wèntí	question, problem	29
wŏ	我	(代)	wŏ	I, me	13
	我們	(代)	wŏmĕn	we, us	15
wŭ	五	(數)	wŭ	five	22

X

xī	喜欢	(动)	xǐhuǎn	to like, to be fond of	20
xià	下边兒	(名)	xiàbiānr	below, the following	23
	下(星期)		xià(xīngqī)	next (week)	27
	下(課)		xià(kè)	the class is over, after class	28
xiān	先生	(名)	xiānshēng	teacher, Mr., sir	13
xiàn	現在	(名)	xiànzài	now, at present	25
xiǎng	想	(动、能动)	xiǎng	to think, to want, to intend	29
xiǎo	小	(形)	xiǎo	little, small	14
	小說兒	(名)	xiǎoshuōr 〔本〕	novel	29
xiē	些	(量)	xiē	some	19
xiě	写	(动)	xiě	to write	21
xiè	謝謝		xièxiè	to thank, thanks	29
xīn	新	(形)	xīn	new	14
xīng	星期	(名)	xīngqī	week	25
xiū	休息	(动)	xiūxi	rest, to take a rest	28
xué	学生	(名)	xuéshēng	student	13
	学習	(动)	xuéxí	to study	16
	学	(动)	xué	to learn, to study	19
	学校	(名)	xuéxiào	school	20

Y

yào	要	(动、能动)	yào	to want, should	26
yě	也	(副)	yě	also, too	17
yī	一	(数)	yī	a, one	14
yí	一定	(副)	yídìng	certainly	21
yǐ	椅子	(名)	yǐzi 〔把〕	chair	17
	以后	(副)	yǐhòu	afterwards	26
	已經	(副)	yǐjing	already	28

yì	一起	(副)	yìqǐ	together	20
yīng	应該	(能动)	yīnggāi	should, ought	26
yòng	用	(动)	yòng	to use	26
yǒu	有	(动)	yǒu	to have	16
	有意思		yǒuyìsi	interesting	17
yǔ	語法	(名)	yǔfǎ	grammar	27
yuè	月	(名)	yuè	month	25

Z

zá	杂誌	(名)	zázhì 〔本〕	magazine	17
zài	在	(动)	zài	to be, on, in, at	23
zǎo	早	(形)	zǎo	early	21
zěn	怎么样	(代)	zěnmǒyàng	how (is it)	19
zhāng	張	(量)	zhāng	(a measure word)	14
zhè	这兒	(代)	zhèr	here	20
	这里	(代)	zhèli	here	20
zhèi	这	(代)	zhèi, zhè	this	13
zhǐ	枝	(量)	zhī	(a measure word)	15
	知道	(动)	zhīdào	to know	19
zhǐ	紙	(名)	zhǐ 〔張〕	paper	14
	只	(副)	zhǐ	only	16
zhōng	中国	(名)	Zhōngguó	China, Chinese	13
	中文	(名)	zhōngwén	the Chinese language	16
	中間兒	(名)	zhōngjiànr	middle	23
zhù	住	(动)	zhù	to live, to dwell	28
zhuō	桌子	(名)	zhuōzi 〔張〕	table	17
zì	字典	(名)	zìdiǎn	dictionary	26
	字	(名)	zì	character	28
zuó	昨天	(名)	zuótiǎn	yesterday	27
zuò	作	(动)	zuò	to do, to make, to work, to be	23

A CATALOG OF SELECTED
DOVER BOOKS
IN ALL FIELDS OF INTEREST

A CATALOG OF SELECTED DOVER
BOOKS IN ALL FIELDS OF INTEREST

CONCERNING THE SPIRITUAL IN ART, Wassily Kandinsky. Pioneering work by father of abstract art. Thoughts on color theory, nature of art. Analysis of earlier masters. 12 illustrations. 80pp. of text. 5⅜ x 8½.   23411-8 Pa. $4.95

ANIMALS: 1,419 Copyright-Free Illustrations of Mammals, Birds, Fish, Insects, etc., Jim Harter (ed.). Clear wood engravings present, in extremely lifelike poses, over 1,000 species of animals. One of the most extensive pictorial sourcebooks of its kind. Captions. Index. 284pp. 9 x 12.   23766-4 Pa. $14.95

CELTIC ART: The Methods of Construction, George Bain. Simple geometric techniques for making Celtic interlacements, spirals, Kells-type initials, animals, humans, etc. Over 500 illustrations. 160pp. 9 x 12. (USO)   22923-8 Pa. $9.95

AN ATLAS OF ANATOMY FOR ARTISTS, Fritz Schider. Most thorough reference work on art anatomy in the world. Hundreds of illustrations, including selections from works by Vesalius, Leonardo, Goya, Ingres, Michelangelo, others. 593 illustrations. 192pp. 7⅛ x 10¼.   20241-0 Pa. $9.95

CELTIC HAND STROKE-BY-STROKE (Irish Half-Uncial from "The Book of Kells"): An Arthur Baker Calligraphy Manual, Arthur Baker. Complete guide to creating each letter of the alphabet in distinctive Celtic manner. Covers hand position, strokes, pens, inks, paper, more. Illustrated. 48pp. 8¼ x 11.   24336-2 Pa. $3.95

EASY ORIGAMI, John Montroll. Charming collection of 32 projects (hat, cup, pelican, piano, swan, many more) specially designed for the novice origami hobbyist. Clearly illustrated easy-to-follow instructions insure that even beginning papercrafters will achieve successful results. 48pp. 8¼ x 11.   27298-2 Pa. $3.50

THE COMPLETE BOOK OF BIRDHOUSE CONSTRUCTION FOR WOODWORKERS, Scott D. Campbell. Detailed instructions, illustrations, tables. Also data on bird habitat and instinct patterns. Bibliography. 3 tables. 63 illustrations in 15 figures. 48pp. 5¼ x 8½.   24407-5 Pa. $2.50

BLOOMINGDALE'S ILLUSTRATED 1886 CATALOG: Fashions, Dry Goods and Housewares, Bloomingdale Brothers. Famed merchants' extremely rare catalog depicting about 1,700 products: clothing, housewares, firearms, dry goods, jewelry, more. Invaluable for dating, identifying vintage items. Also, copyright-free graphics for artists, designers. Co-published with Henry Ford Museum & Greenfield Village. 160pp. 8¼ x 11.   25780-0 Pa. $10.95

HISTORIC COSTUME IN PICTURES, Braun & Schneider. Over 1,450 costumed figures in clearly detailed engravings–from dawn of civilization to end of 19th century. Captions. Many folk costumes. 256pp. 8⅜ x 11¾.   23150-X Pa. $12.95

STICKLEY CRAFTSMAN FURNITURE CATALOGS, Gustav Stickley and L. & J. G. Stickley. Beautiful, functional furniture in two authentic catalogs from 1910. 594 illustrations, including 277 photos, show settles, rockers, armchairs, reclining chairs, bookcases, desks, tables. 183pp. 6½ x 9¼.   23838-5 Pa. $11.95

AMERICAN LOCOMOTIVES IN HISTORIC PHOTOGRAPHS: 1858 to 1949, Ron Ziel (ed.). A rare collection of 126 meticulously detailed official photographs, called "builder portraits," of American locomotives that majestically chronicle the rise of steam locomotive power in America. Introduction. Detailed captions. xi + 129pp. 9 x 12.   27393-8 Pa. $12.95

AMERICA'S LIGHTHOUSES: An Illustrated History, Francis Ross Holland, Jr. Delightfully written, profusely illustrated fact-filled survey of over 200 American lighthouses since 1716. History, anecdotes, technological advances, more. 240pp. 8 x 10¾.
                                                                    25576-X Pa. $12.95

TOWARDS A NEW ARCHITECTURE, Le Corbusier. Pioneering manifesto by founder of "International School." Technical and aesthetic theories, views of industry, economics, relation of form to function, "mass-production split" and much more. Profusely illustrated. 320pp. 6⅛ x 9¼. (USO)   25023-7 Pa. $9.95

HOW THE OTHER HALF LIVES, Jacob Riis. Famous journalistic record, exposing poverty and degradation of New York slums around 1900, by major social reformer. 100 striking and influential photographs. 233pp. 10 x 7⅞.
                                                                    22012-5 Pa. $11.95

FRUIT KEY AND TWIG KEY TO TREES AND SHRUBS, William M. Harlow. One of the handiest and most widely used identification aids. Fruit key covers 120 deciduous and evergreen species; twig key 160 deciduous species. Easily used. Over 300 photographs. 126pp. 5⅜ x 8½.   20511-8 Pa. $3.95

COMMON BIRD SONGS, Dr. Donald J. Borror. Songs of 60 most common U.S. birds: robins, sparrows, cardinals, bluejays, finches, more–arranged in order of increasing complexity. Up to 9 variations of songs of each species.
                                                         Cassette and manual 99911-4 $8.95

ORCHIDS AS HOUSE PLANTS, Rebecca Tyson Northen. Grow cattleyas and many other kinds of orchids–in a window, in a case, or under artificial light. 63 illustrations. 148pp. 5⅜ x 8½.   23261-1 Pa. $4.95

MONSTER MAZES, Dave Phillips. Masterful mazes at four levels of difficulty. Avoid deadly perils and evil creatures to find magical treasures. Solutions for all 32 exciting illustrated puzzles. 48pp. 8¼ x 11.   26005-4 Pa. $2.95

MOZART'S DON GIOVANNI (DOVER OPERA LIBRETTO SERIES), Wolfgang Amadeus Mozart. Introduced and translated by Ellen H. Bleiler. Standard Italian libretto, with complete English translation. Convenient and thoroughly portable–an ideal companion for reading along with a recording or the performance itself. Introduction. List of characters. Plot summary. 121pp. 5¼ x 8½.
                                                                    24944-1 Pa. $3.95

TECHNICAL MANUAL AND DICTIONARY OF CLASSICAL BALLET, Gail Grant. Defines, explains, comments on steps, movements, poses and concepts. 15-page pictorial section. Basic book for student, viewer. 127pp. 5⅜ x 8½.
                                                                    21843-0 Pa. $4.95

BRASS INSTRUMENTS: Their History and Development, Anthony Baines. Authoritative, updated survey of the evolution of trumpets, trombones, bugles, cornets, French horns, tubas and other brass wind instruments. Over 140 illustrations and 48 music examples. Corrected and updated by author. New preface. Bibliography. 320pp. 5⅜ x 8½.   27574-4 Pa. $9.95

HOLLYWOOD GLAMOR PORTRAITS, John Kobal (ed.). 145 photos from 1926-49. Harlow, Gable, Bogart, Bacall; 94 stars in all. Full background on photographers, technical aspects. 160pp. 8⅜ x 11¼.   23352-9 Pa. $12.95

MAX AND MORITZ, Wilhelm Busch. Great humor classic in both German and English. Also 10 other works: "Cat and Mouse," "Plisch and Plumm," etc. 216pp. 5⅜ x 8½.
20181-3 Pa. $6.95

THE RAVEN AND OTHER FAVORITE POEMS, Edgar Allan Poe. Over 40 of the author's most memorable poems: "The Bells," "Ulalume," "Israfel," "To Helen," "The Conqueror Worm," "Eldorado," "Annabel Lee," many more. Alphabetic lists of titles and first lines. 64pp. 5³⁄₁₆ x 8¼.   26685-0 Pa. $1.00

PERSONAL MEMOIRS OF U. S. GRANT, Ulysses Simpson Grant. Intelligent, deeply moving firsthand account of Civil War campaigns, considered by many the finest military memoirs ever written. Includes letters, historic photographs, maps and more. 528pp. 6⅛ x 9¼.   28587-1 Pa. $12.95

AMULETS AND SUPERSTITIONS, E. A. Wallis Budge. Comprehensive discourse on origin, powers of amulets in many ancient cultures: Arab, Persian Babylonian, Assyrian, Egyptian, Gnostic, Hebrew, Phoenician, Syriac, etc. Covers cross, swastika, crucifix, seals, rings, stones, etc. 584pp. 5⅜ x 8½. 23573-4 Pa. $12.95

RUSSIAN STORIES/PYCCKNE PACCKA3bl: A Dual-Language Book, edited by Gleb Struve. Twelve tales by such masters as Chekhov, Tolstoy, Dostoevsky, Pushkin, others. Excellent word-for-word English translations on facing pages, plus teaching and study aids, Russian/English vocabulary, biographical/critical introductions, more. 416pp. 5⅜ x 8½.   26244-8 Pa. $9.95

PHILADELPHIA THEN AND NOW: 60 Sites Photographed in the Past and Present, Kenneth Finkel and Susan Oyama. Rare photographs of City Hall, Logan Square, Independence Hall, Betsy Ross House, other landmarks juxtaposed with contemporary views. Captures changing face of historic city. Introduction. Captions. 128pp. 8¼ x 11.   25790-8 Pa. $9.95

AIA ARCHITECTURAL GUIDE TO NASSAU AND SUFFOLK COUNTIES, LONG ISLAND, The American Institute of Architects, Long Island Chapter, and the Society for the Preservation of Long Island Antiquities. Comprehensive, well-researched and generously illustrated volume brings to life over three centuries of Long Island's great architectural heritage. More than 240 photographs with authoritative, extensively detailed captions. 176pp. 8¼ x 11.   26946-9 Pa. $14.95

NORTH AMERICAN INDIAN LIFE: Customs and Traditions of 23 Tribes, Elsie Clews Parsons (ed.). 27 fictionalized essays by noted anthropologists examine religion, customs, government, additional facets of life among the Winnebago, Crow, Zuni, Eskimo, other tribes. 480pp. 6⅛ x 9¼.   27377-6 Pa. $10.95

FRANK LLOYD WRIGHT'S HOLLYHOCK HOUSE, Donald Hoffmann. Lavishly illustrated, carefully documented study of one of Wright's most controversial residential designs. Over 120 photographs, floor plans, elevations, etc. Detailed perceptive text by noted Wright scholar. Index. 128pp. 9¼ x 10¾. 27133-1 Pa. $11.95

THE MALE AND FEMALE FIGURE IN MOTION: 60 Classic Photographic Sequences, Eadweard Muybridge. 60 true-action photographs of men and women walking, running, climbing, bending, turning, etc., reproduced from rare 19th-century masterpiece. vi + 121pp. 9 x 12. 24745-7 Pa. $10.95

1001 QUESTIONS ANSWERED ABOUT THE SEASHORE, N. J. Berrill and Jacquelyn Berrill. Queries answered about dolphins, sea snails, sponges, starfish, fishes, shore birds, many others. Covers appearance, breeding, growth, feeding, much more. 305pp. 5¼ x 8¼. 23366-9 Pa. $8.95

GUIDE TO OWL WATCHING IN NORTH AMERICA, Donald S. Heintzelman. Superb guide offers complete data and descriptions of 19 species: barn owl, screech owl, snowy owl, many more. Expert coverage of owl-watching equipment, conservation, migrations and invasions, etc. Guide to observing sites. 84 illustrations. xiii + 193pp. 5⅜ x 8½. 27344-X Pa. $8.95

MEDICINAL AND OTHER USES OF NORTH AMERICAN PLANTS: A Historical Survey with Special Reference to the Eastern Indian Tribes, Charlotte Erichsen-Brown. Chronological historical citations document 500 years of usage of plants, trees, shrubs native to eastern Canada, northeastern U.S. Also complete identifying information. 343 illustrations. 544pp. 6½ x 9¼. 25951-X Pa. $12.95

STORYBOOK MAZES, Dave Phillips. 23 stories and mazes on two-page spreads: Wizard of Oz, Treasure Island, Robin Hood, etc. Solutions. 64pp. 8¼ x 11. 23628-5 Pa. $2.95

NEGRO FOLK MUSIC, U.S.A., Harold Courlander. Noted folklorist's scholarly yet readable analysis of rich and varied musical tradition. Includes authentic versions of over 40 folk songs. Valuable bibliography and discography. xi + 324pp. 5⅜ x 8½. 27350-4 Pa. $9.95

MOVIE-STAR PORTRAITS OF THE FORTIES, John Kobal (ed.). 163 glamor, studio photos of 106 stars of the 1940s: Rita Hayworth, Ava Gardner, Marlon Brando, Clark Gable, many more. 176pp. 8⅜ x 11¼. 23546-7 Pa. $12.95

BENCHLEY LOST AND FOUND, Robert Benchley. Finest humor from early 30s, about pet peeves, child psychologists, post office and others. Mostly unavailable elsewhere. 73 illustrations by Peter Arno and others. 183pp. 5⅜ x 8½. 22410-4 Pa. $6.95

YEKL and THE IMPORTED BRIDEGROOM AND OTHER STORIES OF YIDDISH NEW YORK, Abraham Cahan. Film Hester Street based on Yekl (1896). Novel, other stories among first about Jewish immigrants on N.Y.'s East Side. 240pp. 5⅜ x 8½. 22427-9 Pa. $6.95

SELECTED POEMS, Walt Whitman. Generous sampling from *Leaves of Grass.* Twenty-four poems include "I Hear America Singing," "Song of the Open Road," "I Sing the Body Electric," "When Lilacs Last in the Dooryard Bloom'd," "O Captain! My Captain!"–all reprinted from an authoritative edition. Lists of titles and first lines. 128pp. 5³⁄₁₆ x 8¼. 26878-0 Pa. $1.00

THE BEST TALES OF HOFFMANN, E. T. A. Hoffmann. 10 of Hoffmann's most important stories: "Nutcracker and the King of Mice," "The Golden Flowerpot," etc. 458pp. 5⅜ x 8½. 21793-0 Pa. $9.95

FROM FETISH TO GOD IN ANCIENT EGYPT, E. A. Wallis Budge. Rich detailed survey of Egyptian conception of "God" and gods, magic, cult of animals, Osiris, more. Also, superb English translations of hymns and legends. 240 illustrations. 545pp. 5⅜ x 8½. 25803-3 Pa. $13.95

FRENCH STORIES/CONTES FRANÇAIS: A Dual-Language Book, Wallace Fowlie. Ten stories by French masters, Voltaire to Camus: "Micromegas" by Voltaire; "The Atheist's Mass" by Balzac; "Minuet" by de Maupassant; "The Guest" by Camus, six more. Excellent English translations on facing pages. Also French-English vocabulary list, exercises, more. 352pp. 5⅜ x 8½. 26443-2 Pa. $9.95

CHICAGO AT THE TURN OF THE CENTURY IN PHOTOGRAPHS: 122 Historic Views from the Collections of the Chicago Historical Society, Larry A. Viskochil. Rare large-format prints offer detailed views of City Hall, State Street, the Loop, Hull House, Union Station, many other landmarks, circa 1904-1913. Introduction. Captions. Maps. 144pp. 9⅜ x 12¼. 24656-6 Pa. $12.95

OLD BROOKLYN IN EARLY PHOTOGRAPHS, 1865-1929, William Lee Younger. Luna Park, Gravesend race track, construction of Grand Army Plaza, moving of Hotel Brighton, etc. 157 previously unpublished photographs. 165pp. 8⅞ x 11¾. 23587-4 Pa. $13.95

THE MYTHS OF THE NORTH AMERICAN INDIANS, Lewis Spence. Rich anthology of the myths and legends of the Algonquins, Iroquois, Pawnees and Sioux, prefaced by an extensive historical and ethnological commentary. 36 illustrations. 480pp. 5⅜ x 8½. 25967-6 Pa. $10.95

AN ENCYCLOPEDIA OF BATTLES: Accounts of Over 1,560 Battles from 1479 B.C. to the Present, David Eggenberger. Essential details of every major battle in recorded history from the first battle of Megiddo in 1479 B.C. to Grenada in 1984. List of Battle Maps. New Appendix covering the years 1967-1984. Index. 99 illustrations. 544pp. 6½ x 9¼. 24913-1 Pa. $16.95

SAILING ALONE AROUND THE WORLD, Captain Joshua Slocum. First man to sail around the world, alone, in small boat. One of great feats of seamanship told in delightful manner. 67 illustrations. 294pp. 5⅜ x 8½. 20326-3 Pa. $6.95

ANARCHISM AND OTHER ESSAYS, Emma Goldman. Powerful, penetrating, prophetic essays on direct action, role of minorities, prison reform, puritan hypocrisy, violence, etc. 271pp. 5⅜ x 8½. 22484-8 Pa. $7.95

MYTHS OF THE HINDUS AND BUDDHISTS, Ananda K. Coomaraswamy and Sister Nivedita. Great stories of the epics; deeds of Krishna, Shiva, taken from puranas, Vedas, folk tales; etc. 32 illustrations. 400pp. 5⅜ x 8½. 21759-0 Pa. $12.95

BEYOND PSYCHOLOGY, Otto Rank. Fear of death, desire of immortality, nature of sexuality, social organization, creativity, according to Rankian system. 291pp. 5⅜ x 8½. 20485-5 Pa. $8.95

A THEOLOGICO-POLITICAL TREATISE, Benedict Spinoza. Also contains unfinished Political Treatise. Great classic on religious liberty, theory of government on common consent. R. Elwes translation. Total of 421pp. 5⅜ x 8½. 20249-6 Pa. $9.95

MY BONDAGE AND MY FREEDOM, Frederick Douglass. Born a slave, Douglass became outspoken force in antislavery movement. The best of Douglass' autobiographies. Graphic description of slave life. 464pp. 5⅜ x 8½. 22457-0 Pa. $8.95

FOLLOWING THE EQUATOR: A Journey Around the World, Mark Twain. Fascinating humorous account of 1897 voyage to Hawaii, Australia, India, New Zealand, etc. Ironic, bemused reports on peoples, customs, climate, flora and fauna, politics, much more. 197 illustrations. 720pp. 5⅜ x 8½. 26113-1 Pa. $15.95

THE PEOPLE CALLED SHAKERS, Edward D. Andrews. Definitive study of Shakers: origins, beliefs, practices, dances, social organization, furniture and crafts, etc. 33 illustrations. 351pp. 5⅜ x 8½. 21081-2 Pa. $8.95

THE MYTHS OF GREECE AND ROME, H. A. Guerber. A classic of mythology, generously illustrated, long prized for its simple, graphic, accurate retelling of the principal myths of Greece and Rome, and for its commentary on their origins and significance. With 64 illustrations by Michelangelo, Raphael, Titian, Rubens, Canova, Bernini and others. 480pp. 5⅜ x 8½. 27584-1 Pa. $9.95

PSYCHOLOGY OF MUSIC, Carl E. Seashore. Classic work discusses music as a medium from psychological viewpoint. Clear treatment of physical acoustics, auditory apparatus, sound perception, development of musical skills, nature of musical feeling, host of other topics. 88 figures. 408pp. 5⅜ x 8½. 21851-1 Pa. $10.95

THE PHILOSOPHY OF HISTORY, Georg W. Hegel. Great classic of Western thought develops concept that history is not chance but rational process, the evolution of freedom. 457pp. 5⅜ x 8½. 20112-0 Pa. $9.95

THE BOOK OF TEA, Kakuzo Okakura. Minor classic of the Orient: entertaining, charming explanation, interpretation of traditional Japanese culture in terms of tea ceremony. 94pp. 5⅜ x 8½. 20070-1 Pa. $3.95

LIFE IN ANCIENT EGYPT, Adolf Erman. Fullest, most thorough, detailed older account with much not in more recent books, domestic life, religion, magic, medicine, commerce, much more. Many illustrations reproduce tomb paintings, carvings, hieroglyphs, etc. 597pp. 5⅜ x 8½. 22632-8 Pa. $12.95

SUNDIALS, Their Theory and Construction, Albert Waugh. Far and away the best, most thorough coverage of ideas, mathematics concerned, types, construction, adjusting anywhere. Simple, nontechnical treatment allows even children to build several of these dials. Over 100 illustrations. 230pp. 5⅜ x 8½. 22947-5 Pa. $8.95

DYNAMICS OF FLUIDS IN POROUS MEDIA, Jacob Bear. For advanced students of ground water hydrology, soil mechanics and physics, drainage and irrigation engineering, and more. 335 illustrations. Exercises, with answers. 784pp. 6⅛ x 9¼. 65675-6 Pa. $19.95

SONGS OF EXPERIENCE: Facsimile Reproduction with 26 Plates in Full Color, William Blake. 26 full-color plates from a rare 1826 edition. Includes "The Tyger," "London," "Holy Thursday," and other poems. Printed text of poems. 48pp. 5¼ x 7. 24636-1 Pa. $4.95

OLD-TIME VIGNETTES IN FULL COLOR, Carol Belanger Grafton (ed.). Over 390 charming, often sentimental illustrations, selected from archives of Victorian graphics–pretty women posing, children playing, food, flowers, kittens and puppies, smiling cherubs, birds and butterflies, much more. All copyright-free. 48pp. 9¼ x 12¼. 27269-9 Pa. $7.95

PERSPECTIVE FOR ARTISTS, Rex Vicat Cole. Depth, perspective of sky and sea, shadows, much more, not usually covered. 391 diagrams, 81 reproductions of drawings and paintings. 279pp. 5⅜ x 8½. 22487-2 Pa. $7.95

DRAWING THE LIVING FIGURE, Joseph Sheppard. Innovative approach to artistic anatomy focuses on specifics of surface anatomy, rather than muscles and bones. Over 170 drawings of live models in front, back and side views, and in widely varying poses. Accompanying diagrams. 177 illustrations. Introduction. Index. 144pp. 8⅜ x11¼. 26723-7 Pa. $8.95

GOTHIC AND OLD ENGLISH ALPHABETS: 100 Complete Fonts, Dan X. Solo. Add power, elegance to posters, signs, other graphics with 100 stunning copyright-free alphabets: Blackstone, Dolbey, Germania, 97 more–including many lower-case, numerals, punctuation marks. 104pp. 8⅛ x 11. 24695-7 Pa. $8.95

HOW TO DO BEADWORK, Mary White. Fundamental book on craft from simple projects to five-bead chains and woven works. 106 illustrations. 142pp. 5⅜ x 8. 20697-1 Pa. $4.95

THE BOOK OF WOOD CARVING, Charles Marshall Sayers. Finest book for beginners discusses fundamentals and offers 34 designs. "Absolutely first rate . . . well thought out and well executed."–E. J. Tangerman. 118pp. 7¾ x 10⅝. 23654-4 Pa. $6.95

ILLUSTRATED CATALOG OF CIVIL WAR MILITARY GOODS: Union Army Weapons, Insignia, Uniform Accessories, and Other Equipment, Schuyler, Hartley, and Graham. Rare, profusely illustrated 1846 catalog includes Union Army uniform and dress regulations, arms and ammunition, coats, insignia, flags, swords, rifles, etc. 226 illustrations. 160pp. 9 x 12. 24939-5 Pa. $10.95

WOMEN'S FASHIONS OF THE EARLY 1900s: An Unabridged Republication of "New York Fashions, 1909," National Cloak & Suit Co. Rare catalog of mail-order fashions documents women's and children's clothing styles shortly after the turn of the century. Captions offer full descriptions, prices. Invaluable resource for fashion, costume historians. Approximately 725 illustrations. 128pp. 8⅜ x 11¼. 27276-1 Pa. $11.95

THE 1912 AND 1915 GUSTAV STICKLEY FURNITURE CATALOGS, Gustav Stickley. With over 200 detailed illustrations and descriptions, these two catalogs are essential reading and reference materials and identification guides for Stickley furniture. Captions cite materials, dimensions and prices. 112pp. 6½ x 9¼. 26676-1 Pa. $9.95

EARLY AMERICAN LOCOMOTIVES, John H. White, Jr. Finest locomotive engravings from early 19th century: historical (1804–74), main-line (after 1870), special, foreign, etc. 147 plates. 142pp. 11⅜ x 8¼. 22772-3 Pa. $10.95

THE TALL SHIPS OF TODAY IN PHOTOGRAPHS, Frank O. Braynard. Lavishly illustrated tribute to nearly 100 majestic contemporary sailing vessels: Amerigo Vespucci, Clearwater, Constitution, Eagle, Mayflower, Sea Cloud, Victory, many more. Authoritative captions provide statistics, background on each ship. 190 black-and-white photographs and illustrations. Introduction. 128pp. 8⅞ x 11¾. 27163-3 Pa. $14.95

EARLY NINETEENTH-CENTURY CRAFTS AND TRADES, Peter Stockham (ed.). Extremely rare 1807 volume describes to youngsters the crafts and trades of the day: brickmaker, weaver, dressmaker, bookbinder, ropemaker, saddler, many more. Quaint prose, charming illustrations for each craft. 20 black-and-white line illustrations. 192pp. 4⅝ x 6. 27293-1 Pa. $4.95

VICTORIAN FASHIONS AND COSTUMES FROM HARPER'S BAZAR, 1867–1898, Stella Blum (ed.). Day costumes, evening wear, sports clothes, shoes, hats, other accessories in over 1,000 detailed engravings. 320pp. 9⅜ x 12¼. 22990-4 Pa. $15.95

GUSTAV STICKLEY, THE CRAFTSMAN, Mary Ann Smith. Superb study surveys broad scope of Stickley's achievement, especially in architecture. Design philosophy, rise and fall of the Craftsman empire, descriptions and floor plans for many Craftsman houses, more. 86 black-and-white halftones. 31 line illustrations. Introduction 208pp. 6½ x 9¼. 27210-9 Pa. $9.95

THE LONG ISLAND RAIL ROAD IN EARLY PHOTOGRAPHS, Ron Ziel. Over 220 rare photos, informative text document origin (1844) and development of rail service on Long Island. Vintage views of early trains, locomotives, stations, passengers, crews, much more. Captions. 8⅞ x 11¾. 26301-0 Pa. $13.95

THE BOOK OF OLD SHIPS: From Egyptian Galleys to Clipper Ships, Henry B. Culver. Superb, authoritative history of sailing vessels, with 80 magnificent line illustrations. Galley, bark, caravel, longship, whaler, many more. Detailed, informative text on each vessel by noted naval historian. Introduction. 256pp. 5⅜ x 8½. 27332-6 Pa. $7.95

TEN BOOKS ON ARCHITECTURE, Vitruvius. The most important book ever written on architecture. Early Roman aesthetics, technology, classical orders, site selection, all other aspects. Morgan translation. 331pp. 5⅜ x 8½. 20645-9 Pa. $8.95

THE HUMAN FIGURE IN MOTION, Eadweard Muybridge. More than 4,500 stopped-action photos, in action series, showing undraped men, women, children jumping, lying down, throwing, sitting, wrestling, carrying, etc. 390pp. 7⅞ x 10⅝. 20204-6 Clothbd. $27.95

TREES OF THE EASTERN AND CENTRAL UNITED STATES AND CANADA, William M. Harlow. Best one-volume guide to 140 trees. Full descriptions, woodlore, range, etc. Over 600 illustrations. Handy size. 288pp. 4½ x 6⅜. 20395-6 Pa. $6.95

SONGS OF WESTERN BIRDS, Dr. Donald J. Borror. Complete song and call repertoire of 60 western species, including flycatchers, juncoes, cactus wrens, many more–includes fully illustrated booklet. Cassette and manual 99913-0 $8.95

GROWING AND USING HERBS AND SPICES, Milo Miloradovich. Versatile handbook provides all the information needed for cultivation and use of all the herbs and spices available in North America. 4 illustrations. Index. Glossary. 236pp. 5⅜ x 8½. 25058-X Pa. $6.95

BIG BOOK OF MAZES AND LABYRINTHS, Walter Shepherd. 50 mazes and labyrinths in all–classical, solid, ripple, and more–in one great volume. Perfect inexpensive puzzler for clever youngsters. Full solutions. 112pp. 8⅛ x 11. 22951-3 Pa. $4.95

CATALOG OF DOVER BOOKS

ANATOMY: A Complete Guide for Artists, Joseph Sheppard. A master of figure drawing shows artists how to render human anatomy convincingly. Over 460 illustrations. 224pp. 8⅜ x 11¼. 27279-6 Pa. $11.95

MEDIEVAL CALLIGRAPHY: Its History and Technique, Marc Drogin. Spirited history, comprehensive instruction manual covers 13 styles (ca. 4th century thru 15th). Excellent photographs; directions for duplicating medieval techniques with modern tools. 224pp. 8⅜ x 11¼. 26142-5 Pa. $12.95

DRIED FLOWERS: How to Prepare Them, Sarah Whitlock and Martha Rankin. Complete instructions on how to use silica gel, meal and borax, perlite aggregate, sand and borax, glycerine and water to create attractive permanent flower arrangements. 12 illustrations. 32pp. 5⅜ x 8½. 21802-3 Pa. $1.00

EASY-TO-MAKE BIRD FEEDERS FOR WOODWORKERS, Scott D. Campbell. Detailed, simple-to-use guide for designing, constructing, caring for and using feeders. Text, illustrations for 12 classic and contemporary designs. 96pp. 5⅜ x 8½. 25847-5 Pa. $2.95

SCOTTISH WONDER TALES FROM MYTH AND LEGEND, Donald A. Mackenzie. 16 lively tales tell of giants rumbling down mountainsides, of a magic wand that turns stone pillars into warriors, of gods and goddesses, evil hags, powerful forces and more. 240pp. 5⅜ x 8½. 29677-6 Pa. $6.95

THE HISTORY OF UNDERCLOTHES, C. Willett Cunnington and Phyllis Cunnington. Fascinating, well-documented survey covering six centuries of English undergarments, enhanced with over 100 illustrations: 12th-century laced-up bodice, footed long drawers (1795), 19th-century bustles, 19th-century corsets for men, Victorian "bust improvers," much more. 272pp. 5⅜ x 8½. 27124-2 Pa. $9.95

ARTS AND CRAFTS FURNITURE: The Complete Brooks Catalog of 1912, Brooks Manufacturing Co. Photos and detailed descriptions of more than 150 now very collectible furniture designs from the Arts and Crafts movement depict davenports, settees, buffets, desks, tables, chairs, bedsteads, dressers and more, all built of solid, quarter-sawed oak. Invaluable for students and enthusiasts of antiques, Americana and the decorative arts. 80pp. 6½ x 9¼. 27471-3 Pa. $8.95

HOW WE INVENTED THE AIRPLANE: An Illustrated History, Orville Wright. Fascinating firsthand account covers early experiments, construction of planes and motors, first flights, much more. Introduction and commentary by Fred C. Kelly. 76 photographs. 96pp. 8¼ x 11. 25662-6 Pa. $8.95

THE ARTS OF THE SAILOR: Knotting, Splicing and Ropework, Hervey Garrett Smith. Indispensable shipboard reference covers tools, basic knots and useful hitches; handsewing and canvas work, more. Over 100 illustrations. Delightful reading for sea lovers. 256pp. 5⅜ x 8½. 26440-8 Pa. $7.95

FRANK LLOYD WRIGHT'S FALLINGWATER: The House and Its History, Second, Revised Edition, Donald Hoffmann. A total revision—both in text and illustrations—of the standard document on Fallingwater, the boldest, most personal architectural statement of Wright's mature years, updated with valuable new material from the recently opened Frank Lloyd Wright Archives. "Fascinating"—*The New York Times*. 116 illustrations. 128pp. 9¼ x 10¾. 27430-6 Pa. $11.95

PIANO TUNING, J. Cree Fischer. Clearest, best book for beginner, amateur. Simple repairs, raising dropped notes, tuning by easy method of flattened fifths. No previous skills needed. 4 illustrations. 201pp. 5⅜ x 8½. 23267-0 Pa. $6.95

A SOURCE BOOK IN THEATRICAL HISTORY, A. M. Nagler. Contemporary observers on acting, directing, make-up, costuming, stage props, machinery, scene design, from Ancient Greece to Chekhov. 611pp. 5⅜ x 8½. 20515-0 Pa. $12.95

THE COMPLETE NONSENSE OF EDWARD LEAR, Edward Lear. All nonsense limericks, zany alphabets, Owl and Pussycat, songs, nonsense botany, etc., illustrated by Lear. Total of 320pp. 5⅜ x 8½. (USO) 20167-8 Pa. $7.95

VICTORIAN PARLOUR POETRY: An Annotated Anthology, Michael R. Turner. 117 gems by Longfellow, Tennyson, Browning, many lesser-known poets. "The Village Blacksmith," "Curfew Must Not Ring Tonight," "Only a Baby Small," dozens more, often difficult to find elsewhere. Index of poets, titles, first lines. xxiii + 325pp. 5⅜ x 8¼. 27044-0 Pa. $8.95

DUBLINERS, James Joyce. Fifteen stories offer vivid, tightly focused observations of the lives of Dublin's poorer classes. At least one, "The Dead," is considered a masterpiece. Reprinted complete and unabridged from standard edition. 160pp. 5$\frac{3}{16}$ x 8¼. 26870-5 Pa. $1.00

THE HAUNTED MONASTERY and THE CHINESE MAZE MURDERS, Robert van Gulik. Two full novels by van Gulik, set in 7th-century China, continue adventures of Judge Dee and his companions. An evil Taoist monastery, seemingly supernatural events; overgrown topiary maze hides strange crimes. 27 illustrations. 328pp. 5⅜ x 8½. 23502-5 Pa. $8.95

THE BOOK OF THE SACRED MAGIC OF ABRAMELIN THE MAGE, translated by S. MacGregor Mathers. Medieval manuscript of ceremonial magic. Basic document in Aleister Crowley, Golden Dawn groups. 268pp. 5⅜ x 8½. 23211-5 Pa. $9.95

NEW RUSSIAN-ENGLISH AND ENGLISH-RUSSIAN DICTIONARY, M. A. O'Brien. This is a remarkably handy Russian dictionary, containing a surprising amount of information, including over 70,000 entries. 366pp. 4½ x 6⅛. 20208-9 Pa. $9.95

HISTORIC HOMES OF THE AMERICAN PRESIDENTS, Second, Revised Edition, Irvin Haas. A traveler's guide to American Presidential homes, most open to the public, depicting and describing homes occupied by every American President from George Washington to George Bush. With visiting hours, admission charges, travel routes. 175 photographs. Index. 160pp. 8¼ x 11. 26751-2 Pa. $11.95

NEW YORK IN THE FORTIES, Andreas Feininger. 162 brilliant photographs by the well-known photographer, formerly with *Life* magazine. Commuters, shoppers, Times Square at night, much else from city at its peak. Captions by John von Hartz. 181pp. 9¼ x 10¾. 23585-8 Pa. $12.95

INDIAN SIGN LANGUAGE, William Tomkins. Over 525 signs developed by Sioux and other tribes. Written instructions and diagrams. Also 290 pictographs. 111pp. 6⅛ x 9¼. 22029-X Pa. $3.95

CATALOG OF DOVER BOOKS

PHOTOGRAPHIC SKETCHBOOK OF THE CIVIL WAR, Alexander Gardner. 100 photos taken on field during the Civil War. Famous shots of Manassas Harper's Ferry, Lincoln, Richmond, slave pens, etc. 244pp. 10⅝ x 8¼. 22731-6 Pa. $9.95

FIVE ACRES AND INDEPENDENCE, Maurice G. Kains. Great back-to-the-land classic explains basics of self-sufficient farming. The one book to get. 95 illustrations. 397pp. 5⅜ x 8½. 20974-1 Pa. $7.95

SONGS OF EASTERN BIRDS, Dr. Donald J. Borror. Songs and calls of 60 species most common to eastern U.S.: warblers, woodpeckers, flycatchers, thrushes, larks, many more in high-quality recording. Cassette and manual 99912-2 $9.95

A MODERN HERBAL, Margaret Grieve. Much the fullest, most exact, most useful compilation of herbal material. Gigantic alphabetical encyclopedia, from aconite to zedoary, gives botanical information, medical properties, folklore, economic uses, much else. Indispensable to serious reader. 161 illustrations. 888pp. 6½ x 9¼. 2-vol. set. (USO) Vol. I: 22798-7 Pa. $9.95
Vol. II: 22799-5 Pa. $9.95

HIDDEN TREASURE MAZE BOOK, Dave Phillips. Solve 34 challenging mazes accompanied by heroic tales of adventure. Evil dragons, people-eating plants, blood-thirsty giants, many more dangerous adversaries lurk at every twist and turn. 34 mazes, stories, solutions. 48pp. 8¼ x 11. 24566-7 Pa. $2.95

LETTERS OF W. A. MOZART, Wolfgang A. Mozart. Remarkable letters show bawdy wit, humor, imagination, musical insights, contemporary musical world; includes some letters from Leopold Mozart. 276pp. 5⅜ x 8½. 22859-2 Pa. $7.95

BASIC PRINCIPLES OF CLASSICAL BALLET, Agrippina Vaganova. Great Russian theoretician, teacher explains methods for teaching classical ballet. 118 illustrations. 175pp. 5⅜ x 8½. 22036-2 Pa. $5.95

THE JUMPING FROG, Mark Twain. Revenge edition. The original story of The Celebrated Jumping Frog of Calaveras County, a hapless French translation, and Twain's hilarious "retranslation" from the French. 12 illustrations. 66pp. 5⅜ x 8½. 22686-7 Pa. $3.95

BEST REMEMBERED POEMS, Martin Gardner (ed.). The 126 poems in this superb collection of 19th- and 20th-century British and American verse range from Shelley's "To a Skylark" to the impassioned "Renascence" of Edna St. Vincent Millay and to Edward Lear's whimsical "The Owl and the Pussycat." 224pp. 5⅜ x 8½. 27165-X Pa. $5.95

COMPLETE SONNETS, William Shakespeare. Over 150 exquisite poems deal with love, friendship, the tyranny of time, beauty's evanescence, death and other themes in language of remarkable power, precision and beauty. Glossary of archaic terms. 80pp. 5³⁄₁₆ x 8¼. 26686-9 Pa. $1.00

BODIES IN A BOOKSHOP, R. T. Campbell. Challenging mystery of blackmail and murder with ingenious plot and superbly drawn characters. In the best tradition of British suspense fiction. 192pp. 5⅜ x 8½. 24720-1 Pa. $6.95

THE INFLUENCE OF SEA POWER UPON HISTORY, 1660–1783, A. T. Mahan. Influential classic of naval history and tactics still used as text in war colleges. First paperback edition. 4 maps. 24 battle plans. 640pp. 5⅜ x 8½. 25509-3 Pa. $14.95

THE STORY OF THE TITANIC AS TOLD BY ITS SURVIVORS, Jack Winocour (ed.). What it was really like. Panic, despair, shocking inefficiency, and a little heroism. More thrilling than any fictional account. 26 illustrations. 320pp. 5⅜ x 8½. 20610-6 Pa. $8.95

FAIRY AND FOLK TALES OF THE IRISH PEASANTRY, William Butler Yeats (ed.). Treasury of 64 tales from the twilight world of Celtic myth and legend: "The Soul Cages," "The Kildare Pooka," "King O'Toole and his Goose," many more. Introduction and Notes by W. B. Yeats. 352pp. 5⅜ x 8½. 26941-8 Pa. $8.95

BUDDHIST MAHAYANA TEXTS, E. B. Cowell and Others (eds.). Superb, accurate translations of basic documents in Mahayana Buddhism, highly important in history of religions. The Buddha-karita of Asvaghosha, Larger Sukhavativyuha, more. 448pp. 5⅜ x 8½. 25552-2 Pa. $12.95

ONE TWO THREE . . . INFINITY: Facts and Speculations of Science, George Gamow. Great physicist's fascinating, readable overview of contemporary science: number theory, relativity, fourth dimension, entropy, genes, atomic structure, much more. 128 illustrations. Index. 352pp. 5⅜ x 8½. 25664-2 Pa. $8.95

ENGINEERING IN HISTORY, Richard Shelton Kirby, et al. Broad, nontechnical survey of history's major technological advances: birth of Greek science, industrial revolution, electricity and applied science, 20th-century automation, much more. 181 illustrations. ". . . excellent . . ."–*Isis.* Bibliography. vii + 530pp. 5⅜ x 8¼. 26412-2 Pa. $14.95

DALÍ ON MODERN ART: The Cuckolds of Antiquated Modern Art, Salvador Dalí. Influential painter skewers modern art and its practitioners. Outrageous evaluations of Picasso, Cézanne, Turner, more. 15 renderings of paintings discussed. 44 calligraphic decorations by Dalí. 96pp. 5⅜ x 8½. (USO) 29220-7 Pa. $4.95

ANTIQUE PLAYING CARDS: A Pictorial History, Henry René D'Allemagne. Over 900 elaborate, decorative images from rare playing cards (14th–20th centuries): Bacchus, death, dancing dogs, hunting scenes, royal coats of arms, players cheating, much more. 96pp. 9¼ x 12¼. 29265-7 Pa. $12.95

MAKING FURNITURE MASTERPIECES: 30 Projects with Measured Drawings, Franklin H. Gottshall. Step-by-step instructions, illustrations for constructing handsome, useful pieces, among them a Sheraton desk, Chippendale chair, Spanish desk, Queen Anne table and a William and Mary dressing mirror. 224pp. 8⅛ x 11¼. 29338-6 Pa. $13.95

THE FOSSIL BOOK: A Record of Prehistoric Life, Patricia V. Rich et al. Profusely illustrated definitive guide covers everything from single-celled organisms and dinosaurs to birds and mammals and the interplay between climate and man. Over 1,500 illustrations. 760pp. 7½ x 10⅛. 29371-8 Pa. $29.95

Prices subject to change without notice.

Available at your book dealer or write for free catalog to Dept. GI, Dover Publications, Inc., 31 East 2nd St., Mineola, N.Y. 11501. Dover publishes more than 500 books each year on science, elementary and advanced mathematics, biology, music, art, literary history, social sciences and other areas.